Elite • 84

World War I Trench Warfare (2)

1916–18

Dr Stephen Bull • Illustrated by Adam Hook

Series editor Martin Windrow

First published in Great Britain in 2002 by Osprey Publishing
Elms Court, Chapel Way, Botley, Oxford OX2 9LP, United Kingdom
Email: info@ospreypublishing.com

ISBN 1 84176 198 2

CIP Data for this publication is available from the British Library

Editor: Martin Windrow
Design: Alan Hamp
Index by Alan Rutter
Originated by Grasmere Digital Imaging, Leeds, UK
Printed in China through World Print Ltd.

04 05 06 07 08   10 9 8 7 6 5 4

FOR A CATALOGUE OF ALL BOOKS PUBLISHED BY
OSPREY MILITARY AND AVIATION PLEASE CONTACT:

The Marketing Manager, Osprey Direct UK,
PO Box 140, Wellingborough, Northants,
NN8 2FA, United Kingdom.
Email: info@ospreydirect.co.uk

The Marketing Manager, Osprey Direct USA,
c/o MBI Publishing, PO Box 1,
729 Prospect Avenue, Osceola, WI 54020, USA.
Email: info@ospreydirectusa.com

www.ospreypublishing.com

Editor's Note

This book is the second of a two-part study; the first volume is available as Elite 78, *World War I Trench Warfare (1): 1914–16*. Although the division is basically chronological, it cannot be rigid, and readers are invited to regard the two parts together as a single source of reference.

Artist's Note

Readers may care to note that the original paintings from which the colour plates in this book were prepared are available for private sale. All reproduction copyright whatsoever is retained by the Publishers. All enquiries should be addressed to:

Scorpio Gallery, PO Box 475, Hailsham, E.Sussex BN27 2SL, UK

The Publishers regret that they can enter into no correspondence upon this matter.

THE 'BIG PUSH'

A T 7.30AM ON 1 JULY 1916 the first waves of 13 British divisions responded to the sound of officers' whistles, mounted ladders and sortie steps, and emerged from forward saps, to go 'over the top' into the teeth of machine guns and shrapnel. As an officer of Württembergisches Infanterie-Regiment Nr 180 described the scene: '... A series of extended lines of infantry were seen moving forward from the British trenches. The first line appeared to continue without end to right and left. It was quickly followed by a second, then a third and fourth. They came on at a steady easy pace as though expecting to find nothing alive in our front trenches... The front line, preceded by a thin line of skirmishers and bombers, was now half way across No Man's Land... when the British line was within a hundred yards, the rattle of machine gun and rifle fire broke out... immediately afterwards a mass of shells from the German batteries in the rear tore through the air and burst among the advancing lines. Whole sections seemed to fall, and the rear formations, moving in close order, quickly scattered. The advance rapidly crumbled under this hail of shells and bullets. All along the line men could be seen throwing up their arms and collapsing... Again and again the extended lines of British infantry broke against the German defence.'

This resolute, profligate onslaught of manpower and material resources followed a week-long bombardment of 1,700,000 shells. It marked Britain's irreversible emotional and industrial commitment to the World War. No longer could England be accused of fighting 'to the last Frenchman', nor would French leadership be a foregone conclusion. Conscription would see to it that no British family or community was untouched by the war, and that all would have a stake in its outcome. It was no longer a war of diplomacy or commerce, but the Great War 'for Civilisation', which could not but reshape society – and war itself. The first day of the 'Big Push' ended with 19,000 British dead and 57,000 wounded: Britain's bloodiest day in history.

Too often the tactics were what Gen.Swinton would call 'fighting the rifle with the target'. As

Two Scottish soldiers with their most deadly enemy: the shell – here, obviously, a recovered and de-fuzed 'dud'. By January 1916 almost exactly two-thirds of all reported wounds were caused by artillery and trench mortars.

3

British troops attack 'over the top' with fixed bayonets, 1916. The huge casualties incurred during the Somme battles of 1916 were not cynically anticipated; the unprecedented artillery preparation was planned specifically to minimise infantry losses, but neither the available equipment nor the techniques for its use proved equal to the task.

Pte.Fred Ball of the King's Liverpools recorded of an attack later that July: 'The fury of our barrage dropped like a wall of roaring sound before us. By some means the signal to advance was given and understood and we found ourselves advancing into the mist, feeling utterly naked. Who can express the sensations of men brought up in trench warfare suddenly divested of every scrap of shelter?... So great was the noise that the order to keep in touch with one another was passed only by shouting our hardest, and our voices sounded like flutes in a vast orchestra of fiends. All at once I became conscious of another sound. A noise like the crisp crackle of twigs and branches, burning in a bonfire just beyond my vision in the mist, made me think I must be approaching some burning building. I realised, when my neighbour on the right dropped with a bullet in the abdomen, that the noise was rifle and machine gun fire, and I felt the tiniest bit happier when I touched my entrenching tool which, contrary to regulations, was attached to the front of my equipment instead of the side'.

The 16th (Service) Bn of the Northumberland Fusiliers were reported to have gone forward on 1 July 'like one man', and were found in several places to have fallen in lines, with 'ten or twelve dead or badly wounded, as if the platoons had just been dressed for parade'. The masses of shellholes were a mixed blessing: men kept stumbling into them, and they slowed the advance, but they provided welcome concealment on a bullet-swept field. As 2nd Lt. Alfred Bundy of the 2nd Middlesex recalled: 'An appalling rifle and machine gun fire opened against us and my men commenced to fall. I shouted "down" but most of those that were not hit had already taken what cover they could find. I dropped in a shell hole and occasionally attempted to move to my right or left but bullets were forming an impenetrable barrier and exposure of the head meant certain death. None of our men was visible but in all directions came pitiful groans and cries of pain. I began to suffer thirst as my water bottle had been pierced with a bullet... I finally decided to wait till dusk and about 9.30 I started to crawl... At last the firing ceased and after tearing my clothes and flesh on the wire I reached the parapet and fell over into our own trench now full of dead and wounded.'

Though the German lines held along most of the front, the carnage was not one-sided. A single German regiment, the Baden Nr.169, took 591 casualties in the bombardment and assault. Even here, on the British 31st Division front where the Accrington and Barnsley Pals were decimated and left 'hanging like rags' on the wire, there were moments when things hung in the balance, and the British had to be driven out with grenades from front line trenches which they had managed to capture.

The Somme offensive would continue intermittently until November, bringing British casualties to over 400,000, in exchange for about 100 square miles of churned mud. Though both the politicians and the High Command had sought a break-through, Sir Douglas Haig would redefine the objectives to fit the result. This had been, so it was now claimed, a 'wearing out' battle, a battle of attrition, which would ultimately lead to victory. Over the years the acknowledged 'sacrifice' of the Somme would become a watchword for futility.

Yet the Somme was not simply a blunder of mammoth proportions: it signified a stage in the evolution of organisation, tactics, and weaponry. Haig may have been a cavalryman at heart, perhaps a reactionary who relied on royal patronage; but he also demanded ever more tanks, and ultimately did not stand in the way of new tactics. He also carried out the national will in bringing the war to a victorious conclusion, whilst politicians both took credit, and distanced themselves from the 'butcher's bill'. Moreover, the main demand for the big offensive of 1916 came not from Britain, but from France, which was already reeling from Verdun. In short, the war was never simple to fight, nor static in its character – nor, given the numbers and skill of the enemy, would it ever be cheap. As Lt.Charles Carrington of the Royal Warwickshire Regt summed it up: 'The Great War on the Western Front began like most other wars... when cavalry were employed on horseback and battles were short and sharp. It then passed into a period of stalemate, when infantry and guns burrowed underground and hammered at one another in prolonged trench to trench battles. In reality the period of fixed trench warfare was not so long as has been generally supposed, the lines were rigid only in 1915 and 1916... During 1917 bomb fighting in the trenches gave way to shell hole warfare, and in 1918 to open fighting... in which tanks and cavalry played a large part.'

The British 18pdr field gun, of which some 800 represented about half the total number of British guns available to Fourth Army for the Somme bombardment, where it largely failed as a 'wire-cutter'. By 1918 the British Army would have 3,000 of these pieces on the Western Front; high explosive shells, new fuzes, and new tactics would progressively update them for the modern battlefield, but their essential weakness as a weapon of positional warfare persisted. The central pole trail limited elevation to 16 degrees, and thus range to about 6,500 yards; and the HE round contained a charge of only 13oz (0.37kg).

Soldiers were changing, becoming an ever more accurate cross-section of the societies from which they were drawn. More importantly, they were less unthinking rifle-carriers, and ever more specialised. They may indeed have been less accurate shots and worse marchers than the Regulars of 1914; but now they were bombers, snipers, tank crewmen, gas specialists, machine gunners, pioneers, signallers, drivers, and builders. A recent calculation regarding the French Army suggests that whereas 80 per cent of the troops had been infantry in 1914, the proportion was little over half by the end of the war. The situation was not so different for other nations. Soldiers were also being forced to be more self-reliant. As *Sturmtruppe* officer Ernst Jünger would notice, leaders now saw little of their men, who operated in ever more scattered formation, and responsibility often devolved to a tank crew, or a single machine gunner. Such men had to be capable of showing initiative rather than acting 'as puppets'.

The tactics of the Somme

By 1916 it had long been realised that lines of riflemen advancing on unprepared trenches stood little chance. The occupants of field fortifications could shoot them down quicker than they could attack; machine guns and artillery locked the front solid, and local successes proved impossible to exploit due to poor communications and the difficulties of reinforcement. Even so, both sides were groping their way towards solutions.

A British Mk.V 8in howitzer under a camouflage net near Carnoy, July 1916. For the Somme bombardment Fourth Army was assigned 64 of these weapons, which could send a 200lb HE projectile out to a range of 10,500 yards. (IWM Q104)

Combat groups with grenade throwers ('bombers') seemed to offer a way to enter enemy trenches and work through them; more open formations lessened the damage wrought by artillery; and greater autonomy at company level gave some tactical flexibility. Two lessons which had been painfully learned in 1914 and 1915 seemed to offer real answers. Firstly, enough heavy guns with enough

shells appeared to open the inviting prospect of blasting the enemy from the face of the earth – with 'drum fire', as Beumelburg's memorable metaphor put it, turning men 'into apple sauce'. The French Gen.Foch was already a disciple; as his memorandum of December 1915 stressed, offensives were made possible by their power of destruction. Artillery was the chief destructive force, which should be applied repeatedly, 'increasing all the time'. By the spring of 1916 he was stating that, 'The completeness of the artillery preparation is the measure of the success which the infantry can obtain'. At long last Britain had the wherewithal for massive preparation. Total production of 18pdr shells in 1915 had been just over five million; in 1916 it would be nearly 35 million. Less than a thousand trench mortars were produced in the first two years of war, but 5,554 were made in 1916.

Men from a battalion of the West Yorkshire Regiment pose – probably in late 1916 or early 1917 – in steel 'shrapnel helmets', and the M1914 leather equipment produced as a stop-gap due to shortages of the Mills M1908 webbing set. The leather equipment was very widely used by 'New Army' formations committed to battle for the first time on 1 July 1916 – e.g. the 31st Division, including three battalions of the West Yorks serving in its 93rd Brigade. The division suffered disastrous casualties that day when assaulting the German-fortified village of Serre, on the northern flank of Fourth Army operations.

The second lesson was that organised mass attacks in successive, timetabled waves appeared to allow the possibility of advance right over the prostrate enemy, who would have no chance to react. In Gen.Pétain's optimistic paraphrase, 'Artillery now conquers a position and the infantry occupies it'.

For the British in the summer of 1916 this doctrine was particularly seductive. Early failures had often been ascribed to inability to marshal reserve formations into the gaps forced by the point of the attack. Scheduling reinforcement in advance, and maintaining constant pressure, was perceived as the antidote. Moreover, many British troops were inexperienced, whole 'New Armies' of Kitchener's volunteers who had yet to see offensive action; and it seemed unreasonable to suppose that they would be capable of complex tactics which demanded independent action.

This digested wisdom became the 'big push' theory as expounded in the British official manual for the *Training of Divisions in Offensive Action* of May 1916. This stated that successive waves thrown into the attack would add 'fresh impetus' and 'driving power' to overwhelm the enemy. Fourth Army's *Tactical Notes* specified that each battalion be on a frontage of between two and four platoons, so that the advance was made in a depth of from four to eight successive waves, each no more than a hundred yards apart. The most difficult part was expected to be the point when it was necessary for waves to pass through one another after those ahead reached their objective. Ideally, entire fresh brigades would now pass over the holding points of those which preceded them, thus swallowing whole trench systems. On the micro scale it was imperative that individuals press on at all costs. Typical orders for 1 July, to 23rd Bn Northumberland Fusiliers, stressed that 'the advance must continue regardless of whether other units on our flanks are held up or delayed', and that on no account should anyone stop to help the wounded.

Though waves and timetables were the backbone of the system, officers and NCOs were encouraged to use their initiative to overcome specific local problems, and there was scope for the inclusion of bombers and skirmishers to precede the main attack. In places initiative took on greater significance. Some battalions of Gen.Nugent's 36th (Ulster) Division, which had the good fortune of initial cover on the edge of Thiepval Wood, were advanced close to the German trenches before zero hour. As soon as the shelling ceased they immediately rushed the enemy, securing a portion of the line. Here close-quarter battle raged with a vengeance, as one Ulsterman recorded: 'The old sergeant kept going till we reached the German lines. With the first bomb he threw the door off a deep dugout, and the next two he flung inside. He must have killed every German in it... I had never killed a man with a bayonet before and it sent cold shivers up and down my spine many's a night afterwards just thinking about it'.

Private Devennie remembered grenades and trench mortar bombs being dropped down steps and through ventilation pipes. Private Irwin recalled an incident in which a man's torso was blown through the air. The result was the temporary capture of the Schwaben Redoubt; ironically, that evening the Ulstermen would meet the troops intended to relieve them as they were finally forced out and back to their own lines.

What was never clear in the British combat system of July 1916 was how artillery would co-ordinate its action with infantry as the battle unfolded. Many commanders, including Gen.Rawlinson, had assumed that more and more shells fired prior to the infantry attack would pacify the enemy to the point of no resistance. It was the same mistake that the Germans had made at Verdun a few months previously.

One factor which has occasioned much comment was the amount of equipment that the British soldier had to carry. Yet not everyone carried the same weight. While many were overloaded, few went into the attack wearing 'full marching order', and precise equipment varied depending on unit and the function of the individual concerned. So it was that an order to the Royal Irish Rifles, 107th Brigade, specified that 'packs and greatcoats' would not be carried, but that haversacks (small packs) containing washing kit and iron rations would be worn on the back, with the ground sheet containing the cardigan 'rolled on the back of the belt'. Every man was supposed to have two bombs and two empty sandbags, and 170 rounds of ammunition; but forward platoons carried wire cutters, while those following up had pick or shovel. Wire cutter carriers were distinguished by a white cord on the shoulder strap. Though 23rd Bn Northumberland Fusiliers (Tyneside Scottish) also abandoned their main packs, they carried three bombs, four empty sandbags, and pick or shovel.

The diary of Lt.V.F.S.Hawkins shows that 2nd Bn Lancashire Fusiliers carried neither packs nor greatcoats, tucking a pick or shovel under the braces of their equipment on their backs. Unit specialists carried no digging tools, the bombers having either a 'bomb bucket' or an improvised bomb carrier consisting of two sandbags tied around the neck. In this unit wire cutters were carried on a yellow lanyard. In a subsequent attack at Mametz the Royal Welsh Fusiliers were likewise committed 'in fighting kit' without warm clothing, and Capt.Robert Graves recalled searching the carnage of the woods at night for German greatcoats. At the other end of the scale, men bringing up the rear carried trench mortar ammunition, barbed wire, and other stores which could raise their burdens to more than a hundredweight (112lbs, 51kg) – proportionately more of these men survived to tell the tale.

Towards the end of the Somme battle Maj.Christopher Stone with 22nd Bn Royal Fusiliers held the opinion that there was actually too much planning and thought put into what the men carried: 'Zero day was postponed over and over again; the plans for the attack altered and enlarged; the attack itself practised whenever dry ground could be obtained, over dummy trenches. New ideas of "battle order", bomb carriers, distinctive badges, etc., were dished out to the men till everyone was heartily sick of the battle long before it began. There was, at any rate, no excuse for not being prepared for it, or of not knowing the various objectives'.

A German sentry wearing the M1916 steel helmet keeping watch through a sandbag-covered periscope at Hill 60 near Ypres, 1916. The helmet, painted a light matt field-grey, shows clearly the lug for the attachment of the extra strap-on frontal plate. It is intriguing that both the British and the German trench helmets, although scientifically designed, resembled shapes popular in the 14th–15th centuries – the 'kettle-hat' and 'sallet'. From the numerals '127' on his shoulder straps, this soldier belongs to Infanterie-Regiment Nr.127 (9.Württembergisches) from Ulm, a unit of XIII Armeekorps.

HELMETS & ARMOUR

Very early in the war it had been realised that many fatal head wounds were caused by relatively small, low velocity fragments. The French Intendant-General, August-Louis Adrian, was inspired by a 16th century idea, and by soldiers' experiments, to design a steel skull cap to be worn under the képi. About 700,000 of these *calottes* were issued in early 1915, and the British followed with an order for 1,000 during June 1915. On the Vosges front the Germans made limited use of a steel skull defence with a nasal bar on a leather cap, developed by Col.Hesse, Chief of Staff to Army Group Gaede.

From such crude beginnings sprang the drive to introduce universal defensive headgear; but armies differed over specifications. The French priority was to protect their men quickly, in a form that was easily identified as French; the British requirement was for a 'shrapnel' helmet which would give the best possible protection against missiles from above; and the Germans' need was for a helmet which protected against low velocity fragments of shell, mortar bomb, and grenade, while covering the forehead and neck. The three major types of helmet were therefore very different, but influenced many nations: the Russians, Belgians, Italians, Romanians and Allied Czech Legion

A Belgian grenadier makes experimental use of Italian 'Farina' helmet and body armour, of crudely improvised appearance. The device to the right is a rifle stand, allowing aimed shots at pre-registered targets even after dark. (Musée Royal de l'Armée, Brussels)

adopted French-manufactured or French-style helmets; the Americans and Portuguese, the British type; and the Austrians and Turks, variations on the German theme.

The French Adrian helmet in some ways resembled a fireman's headgear; it was of light, multi-piece construction, built around a roughly hemispherical skull made in one of three sizes. A two-part brim was fixed to the crimped border of the skull front and rear, and a fore-and-aft crest covered a ventilation slot in the top. The lining comprised a corrugated aluminium spacer, and a 'Cuban goat skin' sweat band with a segmented liner, the segments meeting above the cranium and adjusted with a cord. The helmet was finished with a chin strap and an applied metal badge denoting arm of service. Initially the helmet was painted *gris-bleu*, 'grey-blue'; this was altered to a darker, less reflective *bleu-terne*, 'dull blue', from September 1916. Khaki-painted helmets were worn by colonial troops. The Adrian was not of good ballistic quality, being of relatively poor metal, weakened by the perforations in the bowl. British testers reckoned that it might stop three shrapnel balls out of four. Against this had to be set the fact that the first helmets were on their way to the troops by the summer of 1915, and that three million had been made by Christmas.

The British obtained a trial batch of Adrian helmets, and officers also made private purchases before the introduction of their own helmet. John L.Brodie's distinctive one-piece 'soup bowl' steel helmet was patented in August 1915. Though initially made of mild steel, by October the shell had been changed to non-magnetic, hardened manganese steel – virtually impervious to shrapnel balls, provided that they came from above. That same month the initial delivery was made to the front. The original paint scheme, suggested by Brodie himself, was a mottled light green, blue, and orange which produced a bronzed camouflage effect; but helmets were also painted in green or blue-grey.

The Brodie helmet undoubtedly reduced casualties, but was not without its critics. General Plumer complained that it was too shallow, too reflective, too sharp at the rim, with a lining that was too slippery. These criticisms led to the production of the 'Mark I' model helmet in early 1916. This had a separate folded rim, a two-part liner, and khaki paint finished with a sprinkling of sand or sawdust to matt the surface texture. Initially there were nothing like enough helmets to go round, so they were designated as a 'trench store', to be kept in the front line and used by each unit that occupied the sector. It was only with the summer of 1916, when the first million had been produced, that the British helmet could be regarded as a general issue.

Designed by Dr Friedrich Schwerd, the German *Stahlhelm* was arguably the best of these first generation helmets. It was the result of thoughtful initial specification, and rigorous practical testing, which included placing a selection of German and Allied headgear on the range at Kummersdorf and pounding them with artillery fire. The deep-pressed shell, in six different sizes, benefited from a light and simple three-pad liner system. Though trialled by Capt.Willi Rohr's original *Sturmbataillon* in December 1915, it was not approved for general issue until the new year, and is thus often referred to as the 'Model 1916'. The prominent side lugs of the Stahlhelm were intended to take a heavy additional frontal plate or *Schutzschild* which would render it bulletproof, at least from the front. In the event this proved the least practical part of the system, and saw only limited use. About 300,000 helmets had been produced by July 1916.

In 1918 there were minor improvements to the German helmet which saw the chin strap fixings moved from the shell to the liner band, producing what is usually called the 'Model 1918'. In August of that year another variation with cut-outs to the shell skirt at each side was introduced experimentally, with the intention of improving the wearer's hearing; trials were still incomplete at the Armistice. Originally the German helmet was painted field grey, but the troops improved its camouflage qualities with mud, foliage, sacking covers, and blotches of paint. Official issue white and grey cloth covers made their appearance in late 1916 and early 1917. The famous disruptive 'lozenge pattern' camouflage paint scheme, in which geometric areas of green, yellow ochre and rust brown were divided by 'finger wide' strips of black paint, was not formally announced by the General Staff until 7 July 1918; thereafter it was widespread.

A famous photo of Irish Guardsmen examining a German MG08 machine gun at Pilkem Ridge, 1917, while wearing captured *Sappenpanzer* body armour.

Eye protection remained a vexed question: preserving sight was vital, but all the patterns of eye defence proposed were inconvenient in combat. No army therefore issued visors or 'splinter goggles' as a matter of course, but they were used experimentally, given to certain specialists, or bought privately. 'Splinter goggles' usually took the form of a slotted sheet metal defence held to the head with bands. They were used on a very limited basis by the British and French, but were still being taken seriously enough for American forces to consider their use in 1917. One interesting

experimental type was devised by American occulist Col.W.H.Wilmer, who based his helmet-mounted, sponge rubber-cushioned design on the anti-snow blindness eye shields of the Native Americans of the North-West. The mask used by British tank crews was also essentially a 'splinter goggle' design, with a leather-covered face piece, slotted eye pieces, and a ringmail section hanging to cover the lower face.

Visors were the subject of much investigation, and the French Bureau of Inventions was hopeful of designing a practical helmet-visor combination. Majors Le Maistre and Polack devised models which were either a hinged front to the Adrian helmet, or formed part of a new helmet set. The Dunand brothers worked independent of the French government and invented a number of separate visors before producing a helmet with visor which was offered to the Americans in 1917. Manufacturing problems and the difficulty of using a rifle with the visor down precluded widespread use. The British 'Cruise visor', which saw limited use in 1916 and 1917, consisted of a hanging curtain of mail, but again it was never a standard issue item.

Body armours were widely trialled, but for reasons of weight and cost were used only on a limited basis. Early in the war many companies, particularly on the Allied side, offered body armours and 'coat of plate' defences for private purchase. In 1915 and 1916 the idea of a 'Bomber's Shield' was investigated by the British Design Committee, Trench Warfare Section, which experimented with materials as diverse as steel, Shantung silk, vulcanised fibre, 'woodite', rubber, and resinated kapok. A British silk 'necklet' for the neck and shoulders entered service in 1915, and was issued on a scale of 400 per division. It had surprisingly good ballistic qualities, but was expensive and degraded quickly. The 'Chemico' body armour worked on similar principles, being a sandwich of different materials including linen, cotton, and silk. Limited official use was also made of the Dayfield body shield from 1916, and in 1917 an 'EOB' breast plate was introduced.

The French made some use of commercial body armour, but by 1916 Gen.Adrian had introduced a light metal abdominal defence, 100,000 examples of which were manufactured. Groin and leg pieces were also produced but not used on any scale. From February 1916 very large numbers of shoulder pieces – *epauliers Adrian* – were manufactured and issued; covered with old coat cloth, these were sewn to the shoulders of greatcoats. Issue was ordered discontinued in August 1916, however.

The Germans began to issue a set of silicon-nickel steel armour to a few men of each company in late 1916. This *Sappenpanzer* consisted of a breastplate hooked over the shoulders, to which three hanging abdominal and groin plates were articulated by means of webbing straps. The armour came in two sizes, weighing about 9kg and 11kg respectively (20lbs & 24lbs), and was capable of stopping small fragments, or even bullets from longer ranges. Though effective enough for static sentries or machine gun crews it was too cumbersome to be practical for offensive operations. An improved version of 1918 featured a stop for the rifle butt and stowage hooks for equipment. A total of about 500,000 sets were issued.

Armour shields and mantlets were also provided. Early in the war the Germans attempted to use small hand-held shields during advances.

Later several nations introduced shields which were dual purpose, and could either be worn or used as a free-standing protective 'loophole' when rested on the ground. These included a heavy Austrian set with folding panels and a shuttered shooting hole; and the French Diagre, which was covered in blue cloth and featured a right-angled cut-out in the top corner for use as a rifle rest (see Elite 78, Plate J3). The Italian Ansaldo system consisted of a steel body plate, available in slightly varying sizes and weights, which could be worn back or front, and was capable of resisting a rifle bullet at 100 metres. For use prone a pair of legs were rotated to support the shield, while a slot was opened for the rifle.

Loops were made for use on the ground, or set into the parapets of trenches; according to one estimate the Allies had deployed 200,000 on the Western Front by 1917. At Bethune, Royal Engineers workshops cut loops from standard plates using oxy-acetylene torches; and a type with canvas cover and rear prop was made by Rosenwasser Brothers of Brooklyn for the Belgians. On the German side, the M1916 loophole plate became commonplace; this was made of silicon-nickel steel about 6mm thick, and had a prop and an off-set rifle hole with swivelling shutter. It was proof against rifle and machine gun fire at 100 metres. An even more substantial plate, sometimes referred to as the '1916–17' model, was 11mm thick, with a 'mousehole' aperture, and could stop even armour-piercing rounds. This was held up by 3mm thick 'wings' at the rear which offered some side protection, but at 23kg (51lbs) it was virtually immobile.

RAITS

It is claimed that the very first trench raid occurred as early as 4 October 1914, when a platoon of 1st Bn Coldstream Guards under Lt.Beckwith Smith rushed an enemy sap at Troyon Factory Road. In February 1915 Gen.Sir John French called for 'constant activity' even though the army stood on the defensive. At about the same time the history of 2nd Royal Welsh Fusiliers describes how the commanding officer 'kept alive the fighting spirit' of the battalion by means of 'patrols' intended to deny No Man's Land to the enemy: 'Patrolling was done by an officer who was rarely accompanied by more than four to six men, often by only one. Knowledge of the enemy's wire, reliefs, troops and so on, was sought. The capture of an enemy patrol, a dead man's identification marks, overhearing talk and recognising dialect, aided intelligence'.

Many escapades aimed at snuffing out enemy listening posts ended in fights with rifles, pistols and bombs. In one of the larger skirmishes, on 12 March 1915, three officers and 21 men got close by bluff, using a German-speaking officer, and extricated themselves by whistle and lamp signals. In May 1915 the Canadians were reported as mounting many aggressive 'scouting patrols'

A Belgian grenadier – wearing the French Adrian helmet – demonstrates the use of the British 'Mills bomb'. (Musée Royal de l'Armée, Brussels)

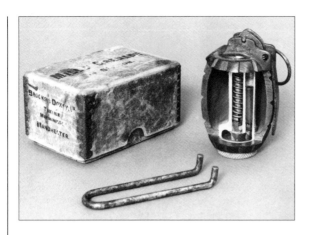

'Mills bomb' – No.5 hand grenade – sectioned for training purposes. Note the spring-loaded striker in the central channel, released when the external lever was freed; a percussion cap at the bottom ignited a four-second fuze connected to the detonator in the off-set channel. Grenades were primed when they reached the unit, the 'igniter set' being inserted through the bottom of the case by removing the knurled base plug with the wire 'key'.

led by NCOs. The 5th Bn Northumberland Fusiliers executed a three-man night patrol in August 1915 to investigate a screen that the enemy had erected, but were sprayed with machine gun fire. Another group of seven went to their aid, and were lucky that there was only one fatality. Such exploits by aggressive units helped to develop small unit tactics. They added trench knives, coshes, knobkerries, knuckledusters, blackened faces, pullovers, cap comforters and muffled boots to the close combat repertoire; but these early raids aimed only at local goals. Trench raids as an official instrument of policy were slower to evolve.

The raid adopted as a model for future action was by 5th and 7th Canadian Bns on the Douvre River on the night of 16 November 1915; its keynote was minute preparation. A copy of the front line was laid out and attacks, the building of 'blocks', the use of bridging ladders and mats for crossing wire were practised. Artillery, trench mortars and infantry were all co-ordinated, while the raiders themselves were divided into two 70-man groups. Within each of these groups were sections devoted to different tasks: five 'wire cutters'; two bombing and blocking groups, each with seven men; two bridge cover parties with three men each; a trench rifle group of ten; a listening post support group of 13; and a reserve of 22. This organisation ensured that once the enemy line had been penetrated bombing groups could attack down the trench in both directions, blocks being established to prevent counter-attack.

On the day of the raid artillery targeted a troublesome machine gun post, and the wire, but this was incompletely cut and after dark the task had to be completed by hand. During the raid one group was discovered by the enemy, drawing fire. The raiders replied with bombs but, being

1917: Canadian troops of the 54th Bn, 4th Division CEF, carry boxes holding 12 Mills bombs and their igniter sets, using the traditional backwoods load-carrying method – a 'tump line' or head strap, worn here over the brow of the steel helmet.

compromised, were forced to withdraw. The other group were entirely successful, stabbing a sentry before bombing dug-outs, taking prisoners, and withdrawing according to plan. Artillery co-operation worked well; throughout the proceedings German rear lines were shelled, but when the attackers retired the guns turned on the sector which had just been raided, deterring counter-attack. The cost to the Canadians had been just one man wounded, and another killed by a 'negligent discharge'.

From this time on Allied raiding became more frequent, and was sanctioned at the highest level. Haig had several good reasons for embracing what he called 'winter sports'. There was pressure from the French: they wanted him to attack, but he protested that as yet he had only a collection of 'divisions untrained for the field'. Raids would both help pacify the French, and bring practical experience without committing the army to a premature offensive. This activity also seemed to offer the prospect of wearing down the enemy and forcing him to keep substantial garrisons constantly alert.

Raids, euphemistically called 'minor enterprises', were now also accepted as the prime antidote to staleness, as *Notes For Infantry Officers* pointed out: 'There is an insidious tendency to lapse into a passive and lethargic attitude, against which officers and all ranks have to be on their guard, and the fostering of the offensive spirit, under such unfavourable conditions, calls for incessant attention. Minor local enterprises and constant occupation during the tour of duty in the trenches furnish the best means of maintaining the efficiency of the troops... Constant activity in harassing the enemy may lead to reprisals at first, and for this reason is sometimes neglected, but if persevered in, it always results in an ultimate mastery, it gives the troops a healthy interest and wholesome topics of conversation, and it achieves the double purpose of raising the morale of our own troops whilst lowering that of the enemy.'

It should not be assumed that the advantage always lay on the side of the raiders. Most 'enterprises' had mixed results, and many were bloody fiascos. At 'Y Sap' on the Somme on the night of 26 March 1916, the 1st Dorsets threw 86 men forward under cover of a mine explosion. Two parties entered the German lines, but the enemy fled, calling down artillery and machine gun fire on their abandoned posts. The Dorsets suffered four dead and 17 wounded, some of whom were initially left behind and had to be perilously extracted. They claimed one German hit. On 2 June 1916, also on the Somme, 22nd Bn of the Manchesters launched a raid into uncut wire which resulted in 30 casualties, three of the four dead being plainly visible the next morning 'tangled in a heap' among the wire.

That very night, not far away at Serre, 14th Bn York & Lancasters made another raid optimistically claimed as a 'partial success'. This comprised three officers and 80 NCOs and men, and was intended to 'gain any information possible... secure prisoners and to increase the morale of our troops'. Preparation was reported to have been good, but the intense

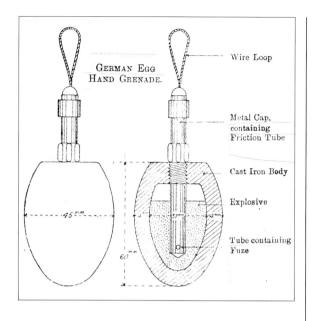

GERMAN EGG HAND GRENADE.

Wire Loop

Metal Cap, containing Friction Tube

Cast Iron Body

Explosive

Tube containing Fuze

45 m/m

37 m/m

42 m/m

60 m/m

Diagram of the German *Eierhandgranate* or 'egg grenade' introduced in 1916. This was small enough to carry in quantity and throw a considerable distance, yet of sufficient power to clear a section of trench.

The British No.34 'egg grenade' which was introduced in 1918 to counter the similar German bomb. It was made in four versions; this is a Mk.III of March 1918. After removing the safety pin the user struck the plunger of the Adams striker mechanism against a hard surface, such as his boot, and a .22in cap ignited a five-second time fuze. The No.34 measured 3.9in x 1.9in, and weighed 12oz when filled – usually with Alumatol, indicated by a pink band painted round the casing.

ten-minute bombardment was insufficient; moreover, an officer and several men were wounded by a 'premature'. A Bangalore torpedo supposed to blow a hole in the wire was too short, and the break-through was made with wire cutters. Then 'the detailed order of procedure appears to have broken down'. Just two officers and a dozen men got into the German trenches, and promptly became involved in a bombing duel. After three minutes the raiders were recalled. Three men were killed and four wounded; the luckiest of these was Pte.McKelvey, who was spotted out in No Man's Land the next morning and rescued by a comrade.

A multiple raid launched by 55th Division on 28 June 1916 in the vicinity of Blaireville Wood, also on the Somme, was suddenly exposed when its covering cloud of gas and smoke was blown away. When they were just 50 yards from the enemy trench, '... He opened out with machine guns, rifles and trench mortars. It was Hell let loose, but someone shouted "On the Kellys", and on we went, but we were cut down like corn. The Jerrys were two deep in their trench, and we realised we were done. Sixteen men answered the roll call out of 76. The worst part of a stunt is always after, when they have a roll call. To stand there and listen to the names being called and try to answer "He's killed" – no one can picture it who hasn't seen one.'

The total proceeds of this raid was one German cap, and a Victoria Cross for a private who attempted to hold off the Germans during the retirement. As the Scottish trench proverb put it, 'Many a muddle means a medal'.

At Arrow Head Copse on 6 August 1916 two platoons of D Co, 1/4th Loyal North Lancashire Regt attempted to raid a ridge occupied by snipers, only to run into machine guns and shelling. Lieutenant Hague and two men were killed, and 25 wounded to no effect. In October and November 1916 the 10th & 11th Bns South Wales Borderers gained 'undisputed possession of No Man's Land' in their sector, but not without cost. In one raid Capt.Charlton surprised an enemy sap and 'disposed' of its six-man garrison, only to beat a hasty retreat before German reinforcements; Charlton and a private were killed, another officer wounded. On another raid Lt.Moore was wounded and was lucky to be retrieved by Sgt.Edwards. 12th Battalion of the same regiment had attempted a 30-man raid on the Maroc sector on 28 September, but were defeated by a combination of wire 45 feet wide, and the explosion of a small mine which threw them into disorder.

According to recent calculation there were a total of 310 trench raids made by the British alone during the battle of the Somme. Near Ypres Capt.Meysey-Thompson of the 21st Bn King's Royal Rifle Corps may well have been correct when he observed that there were so many raids that they only served to keep the enemy ready and alert to intercept them. Captain Henry Dundas recorded a complex raid by 1st Bn Scots Guards in early 1917 which involved crossing two canal lines, only to find that the Germans had already withdrawn, thus avoiding both bombardment and raiders.

Neither were the colonials immune to failure: at Celtic Wood in October 1917 only 14 of 80 Australian raiders would return unscathed. At Vimy the Canadians got into a vicious cycle of tit-for-tat raiding during the winter of 1916/17. In the first three weeks of December 1916 alone the Canadians received reports of 23 hostile patrols, and minor raids escalated into small battles. On 22 December the whole of the 1st Canadian Mounted Rifles attacked with over 400 men; but on the night of 28 February 1917 similar mass tactics met with disaster. A gas cloud blew back over the assembling raiders; the Germans, unsuppressed and alert, proceeded to mow down large parts of the Canadian 54th & 75th Bns, and a total of 687 casualties was reported, including both battalion commanders.

With raids an established part of trench warfare it is not surprising that the dress and equipment of raiders improved. Once

Officers and NCOs of the Grenadier Guards with trench warfare munitions. On the table are a selection of rodded rifle grenades, stick grenades, egg grenades and a German 'discus' bomb; the finned projectile at right foreground is a *Granatenwerfer* bomb. The sergeants hold rifles with (left) the cup discharger, and (right) the No.23 ring attachment. Under magnification it can be seen that, as Grenadier Guards NCOs who are also 'bombing sergeants', they wear two flaming grenade badges on their right arms, and one on the left – that on the upper right sleeve marking them as bomb specialists, while those in the bite of the chevrons on both sleeves were a regimental rank distinction. The 'bomb' of the badge is a padded boss standing proud of the cloth.

troops had been content to discard equipment, fix bayonets, and turn their Service Dress caps backwards – being thus less likely to knock them off, and more likely to be taken for Germans. One A.S.Dolden of the London Scottish recorded that C and D Cos of that unit even made a raid in kilts, with bayonets dulled, and both 'faces and knees blackened'. As experience mounted, however, raiders often adopted a complete new outfit. 'Boiler' or 'crawling' suits made their appearance during 1916; and the Royal Army Clothing Department produced a sealed pattern 'Suit Overall Light Scout' in 1917. Photos of 1918 also show the use of a snow camouflage white boiler suit. The history of 1/4th Bn Loyal North Lancashires describes the night patrol attire as 'boiler suits and cap-comforters' with all identifying marks left behind.

Systematic raiding was addressed by the manual *Scouting and Patrolling* in December 1917. Under the heading of 'night patrols' it recommended that all night activities should be well planned, likely objectives being to gain information; to kill or take prisoners; or to protect an area. All patrollers were to accustom their eyes to the dark before going out, and patrols were to move in parts, leaving at least one man listening at any time. They should freeze when any flare was let off, and should return to their own lines cautiously and by a different route. Depending on how many men were in the patrol, different formations were recommended; and though small numbers were thought best, the larger patrols might include up to 20, complete with Lewis guns. In such an instance scouts would be put out ahead and a box formation of patrollers formed around the gun teams. For small patrols pairs might advance one behind the other, threes in a rough arrowhead. Tip-and-run bombing groups could be formed with a pair of bombers to the fore, and three men behind as a covering party. Equipment was an important consideration: 'Men on patrol should be lightly equipped. A cap-comforter is least visible, the face and hands should be darkened and gloves may be worn. Each man should carry two bombs, a bayonet or knobkerrie, and a revolver or rifle. A revolver is more convenient, but men so armed should be expert in its use. The rifle is best for purposes of protection. Scouts going out on patrol should have nothing on them which would assist the enemy if they were captured.' If all else failed the raider was encouraged to resort to 'hand to hand fighting and various jiu-jitsu methods of offence and self defence', as were taught in the Army Scouting Schools.

In 1916 German raiders are recorded as wearing 'attack order without greatcoat or cap, belts to be worn without pouches'. Perhaps more frightened of being shot by their own sentries, the Germans also experimented with triangles of white linen sewn to their jackets, and with 'white brassards' (see Elite 78, Plate I). Orders from 1917, however, suggest that white marks tended to be abandoned as impractical. Notes of Reserve-Infanterie Regiment Nr.261 refer to the carrying not only of pistols on lanyards, torches, flare pistols, daggers and trench clubs, but also of tent sections for removal of wounded and booty.

Like Allied efforts, German raids met with mixed results. In the flurry of raids at Vimy in mid-March 1917 there were at least two instances when alert Canadian sentries helped artillery and machine gun fire to decimate raiders before they reached their target. Yet in other actions Canadian 2nd Division lost 15 men, and two men went missing from an outpost. The Germans used similar techniques to the British, and could raid on a large scale, as the Americans of Co F, 16th Infantry famously discovered on the night of 2 November 1917. As Cpl.Frank Coffman recalled: 'At three o'clock in the morning the Germans turned loose... several thousand shells. The only thing that prevented our platoon from being entirely wiped out was the fact that our trenches were deep, and the ground soft and muddy with no loose stones. After the shelling had lasted three-quarters of an hour the range was suddenly lifted in a half circle box barrage in our rear to prevent our supports coming up, and 240 Bavarians, the widely advertised cut throats of the German army, hopped down on us. The first raid on American troops was in full swing. They had crawled up to the wire under cover of their barrage and the moment it lifted were right on top of us'.

Two men were killed immediately; a third, Pte.Thomas Enright, was found on top of the parapet with his throat cut and a dozen bayonet wounds – it was assumed that he had been captured but had put up a struggle. Seven Americans were wounded, 11 captured: half the platoon was out of action.

SNIPING

Though a very different activity, the objectives of sniping were essentially the same as those of raiding: to gain mastery of No Man's Land, to wear down the enemy both numerically and morally, and to obtain information. Sniping was more than a century old in 1914, yet the skills were either poorly developed or forgotten in the major European armies. The first snipers were therefore French and German gamekeepers and foresters, Scottish stalkers, and big game hunters, who transferred civilian techniques to the battlefield. It was a game in which the Germans achieved an early dominance, which lasted through 1915.

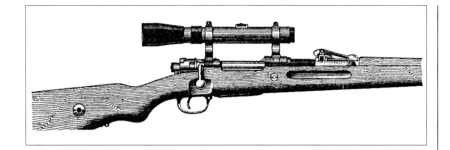

Detail of the *Scharfschützen Gewehr 98*, the German 'sharpshooter's' rifle with 3x power Zeiss telescopic sight. The issue of some 15,000 of these began early in the war, allowing an early dominance of No Man's Land by German snipers in 1915.

The effect, both physical and mental, was considerable. The American Herbert McBride, serving with the Canadians, made close observation of the impact of the enemy sniper's bullet. 'At short ranges, due to the high velocity, it does have an explosive effect and, not only that effect but, when it strikes, it sounds like an explosion... all of a sudden, you hear a "whop" and the man alongside goes down. If it is daylight and you are looking that way, you may see a little tuft sticking out from his clothes. Wherever the bullet comes out it carries a little of the clothing... the sound of a bullet hitting a man can never be mistaken for anything else... the effect of the bullet, at short range, also suggests the idea of an explosion, especially if a large bone be struck. I remember one instance where one of our men was struck in the knee and the bullet almost amputated the leg. He died before he could be taken to the dressing station.'

Medics observed exit wounds up to five inches across, and the backs blown from craniums. As one account so graphically put it, the German pointed bullet 'was apt to keyhole so that the little hole in the forehead where it entered often became a huge tear, the size of a man's fist, on the other side'. Conversely, where the victim was caught unawares at long range, he might be unconscious of being 'sniped'. McBride recalled that unless a long range bullet hit the head, it slipped in with little sound. One Canadian, leaving the latrines, was under the impression that he had scratched his leg on barbed wire. Many hours later the 'scratch' was still stinging, and the surgeon extracted a bullet from the wound.

Initially equipment supply was problematic. In Germany the Duke of Ratibor is credited with initiating the collection of sporting weapons, and the Bavarians are believed to have received their first 'scoped rifles in December 1914. Bavarian regiments were soon supplied at the rate of one sniper rifle per company, rising to three per company by 1916. From Britain and the colonies came game rifles like the Rigby, Jeffreys high velocity .333in, and Ross Model 1905. Yet at first Britain was severely hamstrung by the dominance of the German optics industry. An appeal by Field Marshal Lord Roberts eventually netted 14,000 pairs of binoculars; but as far as sniper 'scopes were concerned, only 1,260 government orders had been placed by July 1915. By this time the Canadians were operating on a scale of four Ross rifles with telescopic sights per battalion, and Sir Max Aitken's *Canada in Flanders* claimed that a Native American, Pte.Ballendine, had already achieved a tally of 36 Germans.

In the British Army the efforts of individual enthusiasts like Maj.F.Crum of the King's Royal Rifles, Maj.T.F.Fremantle, and Lt.L.Greener of the Warwickshires bulked large. Yet one officer more than any other has been identified with the systemisation of sniping and the establishment of army schools. Hesketh Vernon Hesketh-Pritchard, a

German sniper and observer team pose for a photograph in the trenches, 1916 – in actual combat they would obviously not expose themselves like this.

big game hunter and former Hampshire County cricketer, was at first turned down by the army on grounds of age, but succeeded in reaching the front escorting war correspondents in 1915. In his luggage he brought 'scoped sporting rifles, and was soon preaching his creed 'to shoot but not be shot'. His mission was, as he saw it, to 'invent ways to irritate Germans'. In July 1915 he conducted experiments with 'elephant guns' against the metal loophole plates which the Germans were already using, and by August was lobbying Gens.Lynden Bell, Munro and others with a scheme to set up an official sniping establishment.

Appointed as sniping officer to 4th Division, Hesketh-Pritchard was soon in his element, as his painstaking account of a sniping duel on 6 October records. At 3.10pm a German was spotted: 20 minutes later hands were seen fixing a board to use as a rifle rest, which Hesketh-Pritchard observed with a telescope from 420 yards away: 'At 4.15 we could see the brim of his cap, and he lighted a pipe – I could see the tobacco smoke... Then he fired a shot resting his rifle on the board... I think he was shooting at a dummy plate... Then at 4.55 he looked over, his chin resting on the parapet. The rifle was well laid, and I had not to move it more than an inch; then the shot. Later a Bosche with a beard looked over, and this man was killed by the sergeant major... .'

Though there were some spectacular long range shots, moving targets and weather made hits over 300 yards the exception, and some of the best tallies were achieved at relatively close ranges. Men would fall, and their comrades would take cover, scanning the horizon, not realising that the predator was low down and close at hand. The most skilled would crawl out at night to a good position, lay up possibly for many hours, take one or two shots as they presented themselves, and crawl back again under cover of darkness.

Yet sniping soon developed into more than the chilling game of 'assassination'. Battalions acquired dedicated sniping or intelligence officers, and British Army schools of sniping were begun in 1916; eventually not only British, but American and Portuguese troops would pass through them. The work of the sniper officers increasingly focused on teaching and training, inventing, and supplying snipers' requisites. Hesketh-Pritchard developed a 'double loop' which made it difficult to be hit from any angle other than directly to the front, and a system of dummy heads which could be raised and lowered to attract enemy snipers. Major Crum specialised in masks; while Lt.Gray made a board to which sandbags were attached to be inserted into the parapet at night to conceal the placement of new loopholes. Head 'veils' in light and dark brown, which had already been used unofficially, were produced as standard 'sealed patterns' in 1916.

It was also about this time that the Royal Engineers first established a 'Special Works Park' for the provision of camouflage. Apart from huge quantities of netting, screens, canvas and scrim for regular tasks, this would also produce special equipment for snipers and observers. At one end of the scale were complete observation posts, dummy trees, and giant 'Ross' periscopes more than ten feet in length; at the other, painted canvas robes and dummy heads. An unusual item made from May 1917 was the 'Chinese attack' figure; these were cut-outs which could be suddenly raised to simulate an attack, distracting the enemies' attention or encouraging them to open fire. The French, who had already established their own facilities, also had some extraordinary products. Amongst these were dummies representing dead or wounded men and horses. Some would be used as hides, others made to move so as to attract enemy snipers. Later the Americans would embrace the camouflage idea, setting up not only a central camouflage 'Shop & Replacement Battalion' but also one camouflage battalion per army.

On the other side of the line the enemy were moving in similar directions, adopting painted canvas and burlap robes, and head veils. The British *Summary of Recent Information Regarding the German Army and its Methods,* issued in January 1917, noted that 'snipers have been discovered wearing uniforms made of sandbags, merging themselves with the parapet'. Untidy parapets consisting of irregular lines, different

A quiet time for German machine gunners playing 'skat' in a solidly constructed trench near Ypres, 1916. It was in such peaceful moments that a careless man might briefly expose his head above the parapet, offering a target to a patient sniper who had worked his way out into No Man's Land before dawn. Details visible here include a messtin and gasmask canister hanging from nails, and a periscope wrapped in sacking propped on the firing step. The machine gun on its 'sledge' mount is emplaced in the sandbag parapet; the large object in the right foreground is an armoured shield for the MG08.

coloured sandbags, and odd piles of debris were turned to positive advantage to camouflage loopholes and break up outlines. Splodges of dark-coloured paint on sandbags, odd bits of pipe, and reflective pieces of glass were used by both sides to keep the enemy guessing where real apertures and observers actually were. The most commonly encountered German sniper weapons were Scharfschützen Gewehr 98, specially selected examples of the ordinary service rifle modified by means of a turned-down bolt handle and the addition of Goerz, Zeiss or Hensoldt telescopic sights. By the latter part of the war the Germans were operating on a norm of 24 snipers per battalion; yet there was every indication that the British were gaining ground.

British sniping methods were finally codified as part of the manual *Scouting and Patrolling* in December 1917. In defence it was recommended that snipers be found a number of 'battle positions' in long grass, shellholes, trees or piles of bricks, from which they could inflict casualties on attackers, or overlook captured lines. In the attack it was the sniper's duty to work himself into vantage points and ruined trenches. Though good camouflage would be difficult to obtain on the attack, targets were more likely to be numerous.

In trench warfare a system of posts would be established from which the entire enemy front could be kept under observation. These posts were carefully camouflaged with multiple loopholes, and curtains so positioned as to prevent light showing. Once the enemy had discovered such a position it would be abandoned, temporarily or permanently. Working with each observer would be a sniper, 'a picked shot capable of hitting any head that shows itself up to a distance of 300 yards'. Snipers were warned to look out for enemy observers, and smash any periscopes that appeared, preventing the enemy from seeing them and gaining 'moral superiority'. Camouflage, and what we might now call 'field craft', were vital: 'The sniper should make use of veils, sniper suits, camouflage, etc. when available, and scout officers should keep themselves up to date with the latest ideas. The study of protective colouring is interesting and of value; but it must be impressed on the sniper that, however well his disguise may conform with his surroundings, if he does not at the same time learn to keep still, or, move only with stealth and cunning, he is likely to disclose his position. Great patience and constant practice in moving very slowly are required. Disguises may be improvised by using grass, leaves, etc, and by smearing the hands and face to harmonise with the surroundings. A regular outline of any shape attracts attention'.

Sniping at night was thought to be particularly advantageous since most movement occurred after dark, and for such work the Aldis sight with its large object glass was most suitable. Night sights could also be improvised by winding a little white cotton around the ordinary front and rear sight lugs of the rifle. Similarly 'rifle batteries' or rifles set on weighted ammunition boxes could be left trained on enemy sap heads, machine gun posts, or gaps in the wire. They could then be used at any sign of danger, or as a distraction from friendly patrols.

Though textbook sniper establishments might be as low as eight men per battalion, by the latter part of the war many units were fielding a dozen or more. Major Crum recommended from 16 to 24, while the 2nd Worcestershires had an unlucky 13. What had started as 'sport' would end as an enduring feature of modern war.

NEW DEFENSIVE TACTICS

Dispersal in depth – the 'empty battlefield'

Part of the reason for the continued failure of offensives in 1916 and 1917 was increasing power of defence: not only were positions ever deeper, but the methods of holding them more subtle. From ground level this was the 'empty battlefield': single lines of trenches, manned by the whole of the available garrison, had now become multiple complexes, often several kilometres wide, with numerous belts of wire, and deep *Stollen* or dug-outs for reinforcements. Linear obstacles became defended areas, which presented no easy target upon which overwhelming firepower could be concentrated. For the romantically minded this scientific approach to war was a particular kind of tragedy. As Friedrich Steinbrecher put it in 1916: 'The poetry of the trenches is a thing of the past. The spirit of adventure is dead... We have become wise, serious and professional. Stern duty has taken the place of keenness... a frigid mechanical doing of one's duty... . Formerly the dugout walls were adorned with pictures – now they are covered with maps, orders and reports. Formerly the men christened their dugouts... now they are numbered'.

Allied field works were similar, though intended to be less permanent. Considerable planning went into trench systems, but the worm's-eye view was often one of unremitting toil and confusion. A member of 1/4th Bn Loyal North Lancashire Regt reported of 'Beek Trench' near Ypres in 1916 that it was '... a mass of slime and rotten sandbags which it was part of our job to drain, duck board and rivet [sic] with corrugated iron. As nearly every trench in the salient was in like state, and repairs were soon spotted and strafed by the Hun... it will be seen that "Old Bill's" opinion, that the war would only end when the whole of Belgium had been put into sandbags, had much to justify it. Going up Beek trench on a dark night was no picnic. You started along a long narrow alley winding uphill, your hands feeling the slimy sandbag walls, your feet wary for broken duck boards; now and again a hot, stuffy smell, a void space in the wall, and the swish of pumped up water under foot proclaimed the entrance to a mine. Gradually the sandbag walls got higher and the alley narrower, and in places you stumbled where the trench had been blown in and got covered in blue slime... round corners you dived under narrow tunnels two or three feet high, finally emerging into the comparative open of the front line trench'.

The British intelligence *Summary of Recent Information Regarding the German*

German troops living by candlelight in deep shelters. When they finally captured such works, Allied soldiers were often astonished by their elaborate construction and facilities. The German Army built for long-term occupation, not merely for temporary shelter before launching further offensives.

Heldenkeller auf Höhe 151
Erbaut im Juni 1917 für Stab I./422

June 1917: an excellent view of the log and concrete *Helden-keller* ('heroes' bunker') built at Hill 151 for the HQ of I Bataillon, Infanterie-Regiment Nr.422.

Army and Its Methods of January 1917 observed that enemy defences now comprised two, or usually three, defended zones with at least a kilometre between them. Each position was itself made up of three trench lines, with gaps of from 50 to 200 metres, and communication trenches and linking 'diagonals'. When any part was broken into, the remainder would naturally form a 'pocket' able to converge heavy fire upon the intruders. Strongpoints and redoubts in woods, villages and depressions formed the core of defences.

The 1916 German 'Construction of Field Positions' manual *Stellungsbau* recommended that major strongpoints and 'holding on' points could be gradually linked and locked together to form new lines of defence. Dummy positions would be used to mislead enemy airmen. Lines were best laid out so that the forward positions overlooked the enemy, aiding artillery observation. Further back trenches housing the main garrisons were on reverse slopes unseen by the enemy. Individual fire trenches were ideally traversed, and not much more than a metre wide, sufficient to allow a deep passageway behind the fire step, but not so wide as to present a shell trap. A field of fire of as little as 100 metres was perfectly acceptable if this protected the troops. Machine gun positions were to form the 'framework' of the line, a minority of them placed well forward, with surprise increasing their potency. Trench mortars were best placed in their own pits, not in the main trenches, so as to be out of the likely enemy bombardment zone. Some of the details were seen by John Masefield on the expensively won Somme battlefield: 'Whenever the enemy has a bank of any kind, at all screened from fire, he has dug in it for shelter. In the Y Ravine... he sank shafts into the banks, tunnelled long living rooms, both above and below the gully bottom, linked the rooms together with galleries, and cut hatchways and bolting holes to lead to the surface. All this work was securely done, with baulks of seasoned wood, iron girders, and concreting... When our attacks came during the early months of the battle, they were able to pass rapidly and safely... bringing their machine guns with them.'

The German wire – which had 'sixteen barbs to the foot' – was secured to crossed irons or corkscrew supports, making thick webs, 'about four feet high and from thirty to forty feet across'; these were supplemented by trip wires, low entanglements and iron spikes or 'calthrops'. Though the British bombardment on the Somme had been massive it had been lacking in important respects. Its duration had ruined any element of surprise, and its wire-cutting potential had been overestimated. Worse, although just over 2,029 guns had been deployed, only 452 were 'heavies' capable of dealing with deep bunkers. This was a smaller proportion of heavy artillery than the Germans had managed at Verdun.

Some of the latest defensive tactics appeared in the American manual *Notes on the Construction and Equipment of Trenches* of May 1917, just weeks after the US declaration of war. This readily accepted that commanders of sectors 'do not count on holding their firing trenches in case of violent attack, but always have arrangements made in every detail for a counter attack'. It also recommended the provision of narrow 'slit trenches' and dispersed shelters for use during bombardment. The American Expeditionary Force's ideas were a mixture of Allied and German methods, and its troops would initially occupy trenches which had already been dug. Yet *Notes on Construction...* also contained evidence of zeal to the point of overconfidence, as when it recommended the occupation of forward slopes, which were 'certainly exposed to view and bombardment', on the grounds that 'high ground gives a feeling of superiority to the troops and acts favourably on their morale'. Elsewhere it also suggested that about half the trench garrison might be put in the foremost line.

By the time of the Third Battle of Ypres (or Passchendaele – opened 31 July 1917) German systems had advanced considerably. The front was divided into divisional sectors 5,000 metres wide, within which were regimental sectors each about 2,000 metres across. The battalions of the regiments were placed one behind the other, in forward, battle, and rear zones, to a total depth of at least four kilometres. Even the battalion within the forward zone or *Vorveldzone* was not in one line, but was divided up to form a defence a kilometre or more in depth. The sub-divisions within the Vorveldzone included the 'security line' within about 250 to 500 metres of the enemy, in which a mere 50 or so troops would man perhaps a dozen scattered outposts. Behind this would be a

A German *Schutzengraben* or fire trench in wooded country, showing firing steps, grenade dumps, and helmets and bandoliers at the ready.

better defended *Widerstand* or 'resistance' line, where about 200 men including some machine gun teams would provide a checkerboard formation of squad-sized positions.

The last part of the forward zone was the 'main' line of resistance, in which the remainder of the battalion would man two or three trenches. In the event of all-out attack the outlying posts could retire on the main line, and the whole of the area between here and the opposition would be counted a 'barrage' zone for German artillery. Attacking troops would therefore have to struggle through a kilometre of churned ground, potentially under artillery fire, machine guns and snipers, from a variety of directions, before they reached anything approximating a solid 'front' which they could attack. The new emphasis was on individual, but mutually supporting positions.

Reinforced concrete

The increasing use of reinforced concrete was a material aid to stand-alone defences and economy of manpower. The Germans were pioneers of MEBUs, *Mannschafts Eisenbeton Understande* or 'reinforced concrete personnel dug-outs', for which they barged huge quantities of materials down the Rhine, beginning in late 1915. Over time considerable technological progress was made, and early sandwich constructions and the use of heavy rails gave way to new methods such as thin reinforcing rods and precast blocks. The Royal Engineers examined such structures with professional appreciation, noting one particular farm with concrete positions which had been bombarded 'by ourselves and by the enemy for over a month' without yielding, as 'the effect of shell fire on these structures has been practically nil, though the surrounding ground is a mass of interlocking shell holes'. In some spectacular instances super-heavy shells burst next to bunkers, which did not shatter, but settled at drunken angles into the craters.

Some bunkers had embrasures, but many were 'blinds' having no vulnerable apertures, allowing the occupants to sit out bombardments in relative safety; even so, direct hits could cause casualties through concussion, or the flaking of dangerous lumps of concrete off the insides of the walls. When firing ceased the garrisons rushed out to man shellholes, or fired machine guns over the roof of the bunker. Only when the enemy took the position completely by surprise did this scheme become a liability, and then there were instances when dozens of trapped men were captured by one or two Allied soldiers.

By 1917 the concrete pillbox had become the cornerstone of the new

'Plugstreet' Wood, January 1917: men of the Lancashire Fusiliers emerge from a built-up section of 'box trench' onto a duckboard path. This is the rear entrance of a communication trench; in the coastal sector of Flanders, where the water table was very high, fire trenches also had to be constructed above ground in this way.

system of defence, with many small machine gun posts boasting cover a metre and a half thick. Bunkers nestled into folds in the ground, or were camouflaged with turf, rubble, or wood to suit the environment. As Gen.Gough noted at Ypres, 'The Germans had built small but very powerful concrete shelters. These were covered with mud and scattered throughout the desert of wet shell holes... They were impossible to locate from a distance, and in any case were safe against anything but the heaviest shells. The farms, most of which were surrounded by very broad, wet ditches, or moats, had also been heavily concreted...'

Artilleryman George Wear had a similar perspective: 'The bombardments of the Somme... were nothing to those round Ypres. Batteries jostled each other in the shell marked waste of mud, barking and crashing night and day. There were no trees, no houses, no countryside, no shelter, no sun. Wet, grey skies hung over the blasted land, and in the mind a gloomy depression spread. Trenches had disappeared. 'Pill boxes' and shell holes took their place... .'

Fighting for such monoliths could be brutal indeed, with even the *Australian Official History* admitting that having been savagely and repeatedly raked with machine gun fire on the way in, troops were apt to butcher the first enemy to emerge. Once captured, concrete posts were a mixed blessing, since the entrance and the thickest defence were now on the wrong sides. One possibility was to block up the old doorway and blow a new entrance; another was to throw up a new defence in front of the existing portal. Either way it was highly dangerous under fire.

One unit, 1st Bn Cambridgeshire Regt, endured days of such fighting at St Julien in the summer of 1917. The battalion's C Co first seized a trench line and two concrete bunkers, holding them 'like a breakwater' against successive counter-attacks until they were crowded with delirious wounded. Private Muffet distinguished himself by repeatedly crossing open ground to fetch ammunition. The Cambridgeshires' battalion commander ensconced himself in another enemy position: 'Our gun pit, with roof and sides of concrete, was open at each end. To protect us from the German side we had piled up a mound of earth... Over the concrete roof, and for five or six yards beyond the concrete sides, the Germans had heaped earth, which was now overgrown with grass. It was not a residence calculated to command a high rent in time of peace, but at that hour many a soldier would have given all he possessed to stay beneath its shelter.'

Local defence of this impromptu HQ was provided by a Lewis gun dismounted from a stranded tank. Despite bombardment, and the killing or wounding of most in the vicinity, the gun pit held out against German infantry attack. Only when British guns erroneously targeted

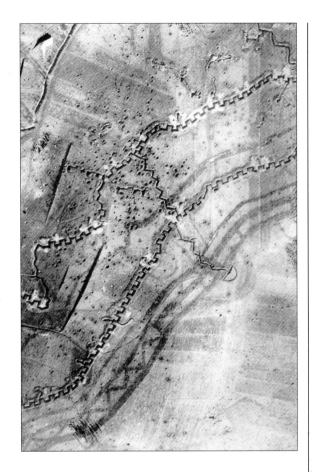

Trenches near Cambrai seen from the air; No Man's Land is at bottom right. This clear aerial photo shows the pocking of shellholes, the stark crenellated lines of two fire trenches, the lazy zig-zag of communication trenches, the shadows cast by belts of wire, and D-shaped advanced posts pushed out beyond them.

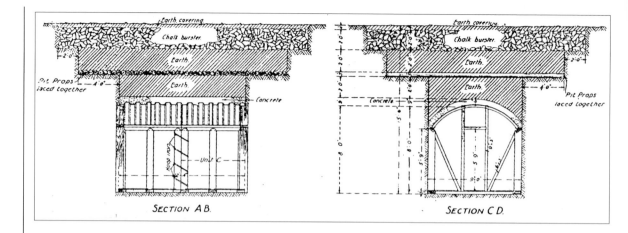

SECTION A B.   SECTION C D.

the pit was the order to withdraw given. Even then Pte.Muffet refused to abandon the position called 'Border House' and leave the two wounded men who remained alive until given a written order. Muffet was recommended for the Victoria Cross, but it was refused.

Not far away, Guy Chapman saw a similar battle given a diabolical twist: 'Then the defenders suddenly saw advancing towards them a wave of fire. The enemy were attacking under cover of a flammenwerfer... When the nozzles were lighted, they threw out a roaring, hissing flame twenty to thirty feet long, swelling at the end to a whirling oily rose six feet in diameter. Under cover of these hideous weapons, the enemy surrounded the advance pill box, stormed it and killed the garrison... the enemy was consolidating the pill-box; but Whitehead and C.S.M.Edmonds, collecting a few men to carry for them, furiously assaulted the place and bombed their way into it. Most of the occupants were killed, and six surrendered'.

As Col.E.G.L.Thurlow observed, the British had a tendency to assume that elaborate concrete works were not worth the immense efforts required, and that they engendered a 'lack of offensive spirit'. They therefore made limited front line use of this material, although some British concrete machine gun positions had been built as early as 1915, and corrugated iron 'elephant shelters' were covered in layered concrete to create 'bomb proofs'. Some individual strongpoints were also well protected. Yet from summer 1917, with their capture of Messines Ridge overlooking Ypres, the Allies were forced to take concrete construction far more seriously. The British Army's first concrete factory, opened at Arques in the winter of 1916, was joined by a second at Aire a year later. The Aire facility was entirely given over to the manufacture of blocks and beams, and at the height of production was making 7,000 and 700 of each per day respectively.

Early in 1918 Aire also formed a 'School of Concrete', and Royal Engineer Transport Works companies were formed specifically to deal with concrete. In addition to block-built pillboxes, 'mix in place' cement was used, as were Moir pre-cast pillboxes with steel domes which were imported to France from Richborough in Kent. Additionally, Maj.Gen.Hobbs of the Australian 5th Division conceived the Hobbs armoured machine gun emplacement, which was produced in Glasgow and transported to the front, mainly for use in Australian sectors.

Diagrams showing how British corrugated iron 'elephant' shelters could be shellproofed using layers of concrete, earth, chalk rubble and pit props: A-B side view, C-D end view. The idea was to make sure the shell burst close to the surface, so that the underlying strata absorbed the shock and fragments.

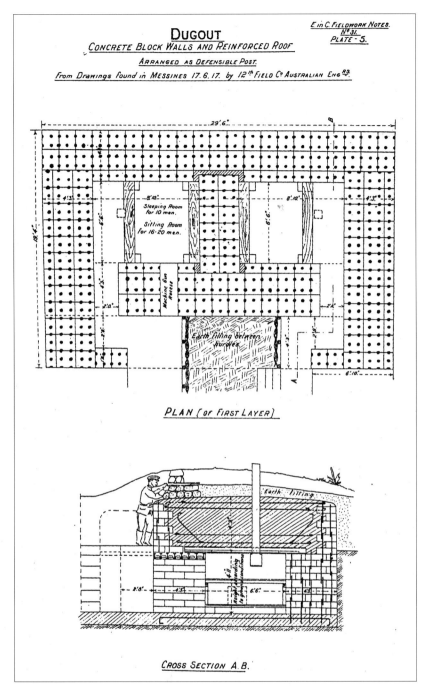

DUGOUT
CONCRETE BLOCK WALLS AND REINFORCED ROOF
ARRANGED AS DEFENSIBLE POST.
From Drawings found in MESSINES 17.6.17. by 12th FIELD Cº AUSTRALIAN ENGRS.

Sleeping Room for 10 men.

Sitting Room for 16-20 men.

Machine Gun Recess

Earth filling between purlins

PLAN (OF FIRST LAYER)

Earth Filling

CROSS SECTION A.B.

Diagrams of the construction of German concrete block bunkers discovered by Australian engineers at Messines, June 1917.

Unfortunately work was not far advanced at the time of the German offensive in the spring of 1918, and both the concrete factories were in danger of being overrun, necessitating the establishment of new facilities further back.

With the turn of the tide in the summer of 1918 the Allies found themselves up against the Hindenburg Line, arguably the best set of works to date, having been constructed out of range of Allied artillery. Here networks of light railways connected the new defensive line with dumps of raw materials and 'mixing places'. Even as the Hindenburg Line was being breached, a British 'GHQ Defence Line' was begun with the idea of forming an ultimate back-stop against any future German advance. This used the latest techniques, including the innovative 'ferro-concrete pancake shelter' in which a hole was dug in the shape of a dug-out wall, and filled with reinforced concrete, the edifice then being capped and the enclosed earth literally 'dug out'.

Though the Allies never managed the concentration of concrete achieved by the enemy, attempts were made to modernise. In late 1917 Haig established a committee under Maj.Gen.Jeudwine, commander of 55th (West Lancashire) Division, to examine defensive methods. Although in the event his recommendations were not accepted in total, GHQ did now issue a memorandum on defence which was little more than an abbreviated translation of German manuals circulated earlier in the year. Where the British were hampered was in unwillingness to give up ground – doubtless because of French sensibilities, and because home opinion would have taken a dim view of yielding territory bought with blood. The result was a relative lack of flexibility. Often front lines had to remain front lines, and the creation of proper 'outpost zones' was not always possible.

Nevertheless, by the end of the war the similarities were greater than the differences. As the preamble to the British handbook *Diagrams of Field Defences* explained, defence systems should now 'take the form of a network of posts and localities sited for mutual support in considerable depth. These posts and localities are to be connected for purposes of command and covered communication on certain portions of the front'.

The handiest temporary strongpoint was the ubiquitous shellhole, as described by *The Organisation of Shell Hole Defences* of December 1917. This appreciated that no two holes were the same, nor should they be, as this was bound to draw enemy attention. Concealment, both direct and from the air, was of paramount importance, all work being 'assimilated as far as possible to the surrounding ground, and regularity of outline avoided'. Alterations were best disguised with mud-splashed waterproof sheets, painted corrugated iron, or other camouflage. Dug earth was disposed of in empty holes, thus deceiving the enemy as to which were occupied. Duckboards or tracks were to be varied or concealed, and any connecting trenches narrow and camouflaged.

A pair of shellholes was usually enough for a section. Typical modifications included drainage, firing positions, overhead cover and wiring. In very wet ground it was recommended that men cut a slot or scrape behind, or in the front lip of the crater, and use the shellhole as a sump to drain water into. In other locations the two holes could be connected so that the ground in between had the effect of a large traverse. In vulnerable locations firing positions would be cut into the shellholes, but permanent three- or four-man weapons pits would be dug nearby, and preferably camouflaged to look like further shellholes. Another method was to pick two or more holes close together, but not in a straight line, and link them with short irregular trenches. Where the holes were deeper than the trenches they became natural drains. Reverse slope shellholes were thought particularly suitable, as they were difficult for the enemy to observe and water would run away naturally.

Wiring was best used inconspicuously and sparingly, on short screw pickets, 30 to 50 yards in front of holes. Even a single strand of wire had the useful side effect of preventing ration parties or reliefs wandering past in the dark and into the enemy. Shellholes which the enemy might use to approach could be denied by filling them with wire.

LIGHT MACHINE GUNS

Despite the existence of weapons which might be described as 'automatic rifles' or 'light machine guns', like the Danish Madsen and the Mexican-designed Mondragon, hardly any were in service prior to 1914. Neither was there any sophisticated tactical theory for their use. In Britain a committee had been formed to look at automatic rifles as early as 1909, and Maj.McMahon of the School of Musketry suggested the provision of one per company, but they were not part of the establishment on the outbreak of war.

In the face of acute shortages of automatic weapons during the first year of war a number of nations took up whatever 'light' guns were available. Sometimes these were treated merely as additional machine guns, sometimes they were given a specific role. In the German instance a small number of *Musketen* battalions were formed during mid-1915, in which four-man squads used Madsen-type weapons with 25-round magazines, primarily in defence. The French, interested in the possibility of automatic 'walking fire' supporting the advance, continued the development of Capt.Louis Chauchat's pre-war auto-matic rifles. The culmination of their endeavours was the Chauchat (CSRG) M1915, a relatively light, air-cooled, highly innovative sheet metal and tubing weapon with a 20-round magazine. Unfortunately it suffered from overheating, poor ergonomics, and frequent malfunctions.

British Lewis gun crew on the bank of the Lys Canal, April 1918. The gunner's assistant, in a dark goatskin jacket, offers up magazines from the steel 'Box Carriers Magazines Lewis .303 inch Gun'.

It was the British who made best progress, adopting a .303in version of the American-designed Lewis gun, and beginning a general issue of four per battalion in July 1915. By 1916 the establishment was increased to 16 per battalion, or one per platoon; and with the removal of the Vickers medium machine guns from infantry battalions to Machine Gun Corps companies, the Lewis carved out its own tactical niche. This was defined in *Notes on the Tactical Employment of Machine Guns and Lewis Guns* as both offensive and defensive: to provide covering fire during the attack; to consolidate positions won; to provide a mobile reserve of firepower; to economise on troops; to defend parts of lines which could not be covered by ordinary machine guns; and even to take part in 'small enterprises' or raids. Although initially viewed with suspicion as an inferior replacement for the Vickers in the infantry, and by no means mechanically infallible, the Lewis soon proved its value.

By early 1917 each platoon would have a Lewis serviced by its own nine-man section, many of whom would be detailed as carriers for the 30-odd drums of ammunition required to keep it firing. During 1918 a second gun was added to each platoon, which, counting the four for anti-aircraft defence, meant that each battalion deployed 36 Lewis guns. On the march the guns were pulled in handcarts, while the horse-drawn limbers which were later introduced could carry four guns and 22 magazine boxes.

In the British cavalry Hotchkiss light machine guns, known to the Americans as Benèt-Mercié 'machine rifles', replaced the Maxims. Fed from rigid 30-round cartridge strips, these were compact enough, though arguably less effective than the Lewis.

In the close co-operation of the Lewis with other weapons was identified a means by which attacking infantry could overcome enemy machine guns. The ideal method was described in the instruction *Notes On Dealing With Hostile Machine Guns*, issued in April 1917. First choice to remove the threat would be trench mortars and cross-fire from friendly machine guns, but if this was impossible the Lewis gun section would work their way forward to fire 'from the nearest cover available'. This would almost certainly attract the enemy fire, allowing rifle sections to move on the flanks. When close enough these would either silence the enemy machine gun with a barrage of rifle grenades, or attack with rifle fire and the bayonet.

Though best used prone, in short bursts, it was just

Officers of various regiments – including the Dorsets, Warwickshires, and an Australian unit – pose with a sergeant instructor (front, centre) while on a Lewis gun course.

possible to fire the Lewis standing up. Edmund Blunden recorded firing from the shoulder in early 1917 when a Lewis gunner fired at enemy raiders, but was killed for his pains. A sling, originally intended for carrying the gun when hot, was introduced in late 1916, but before long this was being used not just for portability but for firing the gun on the move. One of the most dramatic instances was provided by the Australian Corps at Hamel in July 1918. As the official report put it, 'where a tank was not available to clear up a hostile nest, one of the guns of the L.G. section, carried on a sling, and fired from the hip, gave sufficient cover for the remaining gun to come into action deliberately'. The Lewis guns thereby performed 'invaluable work', often in conjunction with rifle grenade fire.

Such effective mobile firepower was soon noticed. As early as 5 July 1916, on the Somme, Gen.von Stein was remarking on the 'large number

A German MG08 on an improvised 'trench mount'. This arrangement was less stable than the 'sledge' mount but much easier to move.

of Lewis guns which were brought into action very quickly and skilfully in newly captured positions'. He further recommended that 'our infantry should be equipped with a large number of light machine guns of this description'. The Lewis gun soon became a prized piece of booty for German assault troops, yet the capture of a relatively few British weapons by no means solved the problem. The Germans had already experimented

(continued on page 43)

BRITISH RAIDERS (left to right) **1: Private, 12th Bn East Yorkshire Regt, January 1918**
2: Officer, 1/8th (Irish) Bn, The King's Regt (Liverpool), April 1916 **3: Private, York & Lancaster Regt, January 1918**

B

GERMAN ASSAULT TROOPS, 1917   1 & 2: *Flammenwerfer* team, 3rd Guard Pioneer Bn   3: Leutnant, Assault Battalion

1

2

3

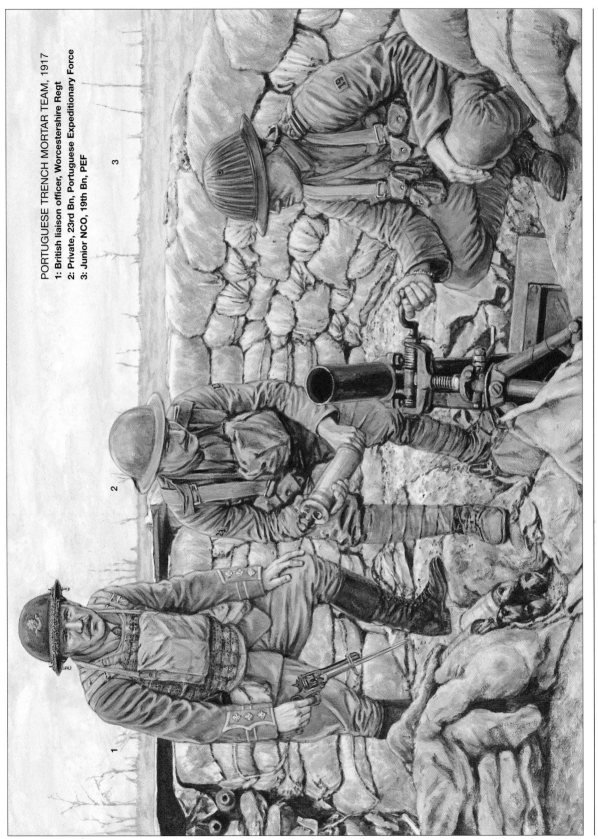

PORTUGUESE TRENCH MORTAR TEAM, 1917
1: British liaison officer, Worcestershire Regt
2: Private, 23rd Bn, Portuguese Expeditionary Force
3: Junior NCO, 19th Bn, PEF

C

BRITISH & AUSTRALIAN SPECIALIST TROOPS, 1918   1: Driver, Army Service Corps
2: Bomber, 1/10th Bn The King's Regt (Liverpool Scottish), 55th Division   3: Lewis gunner, 29th Bn, 5th Australian Division

D

MISCELLANEOUS GERMAN EQUIPMENT, 1916–18 **See text for details**

FRENCH SPECIALIST TROOPS, 1917–18
1: Capitaine, Artillerie Spéciale
2: Sergent, Transmissions,
   8e Régiment de Génie
3: Soldat, MG Company,
   103e Régiment d'Infanterie

F

AMERICAN INFANTRY, SUMMER 1918 (left to right)   1: Private, US 371st Infantry Regiment   2 & 3: Automatic rifle team, 137th Infantry Regiment

GERMAN ASSAULT TROOPS,
AUTUMN 1918
1: Sergeant, *(Bayerisches)*
   2.Infanterie-Regiment Kronprinz
2: Light machine gunner
3: Unteroffizier, *4.Niederschlesisches*
   Infanterie-Regiment Nr.51

H

AMERICAN TRENCH FIGHTERS, AUTUMN 1918   1: Medical orderly   2: Rifle grenadier   3: Infantry company commander

BRITISH PLATOON ATTACK, 1918 See text for details

J

May 1918: a drummer of 1/7th Bn Lancashire Fusiliers shows US troops a Hotchkiss light machine gun on an anti-aircraft mount. The Hotchkiss took the place of the Lewis in British cavalry units; it had already been ordered in small numbers by the US Army in 1909, under the name Benèt-Mercié.

with improvised 'trench mounts' for their MG08 weapons, and now struggled to introduce a light machine gun of their own.

Various weapons were tried, including a Bergmann-designed automatic rifle, but the gun ultimately adopted as standard was the MG08/15. This would certainly facilitate the development of German small unit tactics, but was an uneasy compromise; for while the MG 08/15 retained the familiar Maxim mechanism and a reasonable sustained fire capability from its 100-round belt-carrying drum, it also kept much of the weight. Theoretically a web and leather sling allowed fire on the move, but how practical this really was with 22kg (48.5lbs) of gun, water, and ammunition was open to question.

The Americans, unwisely adopting the French Chauchat and slow to realise the importance of the Lewis, actually came up with one of the best light support weapons at the eleventh hour. The first Browning Automatic Rifles or 'BARs' were shipped to France in the summer of 1918 and first saw action in September: firing from 20-round box magazines, and weighing just over 7kg (15.4lbs), they were particularly handy. As the official report stated, the guns were 'highly praised', and although they received 'hard usage, being on the front for days at a time in the rain and when the gunners had little opportunity to clean them, they invariably functioned well'.

NEW OFFENSIVE TACTICS – GERMAN

To break trench deadlock would require three things: new weapons; numerical or qualitative superiority; and new tactics. Of the weapons it was arguably the light machine gun which contributed most to the return of fluidity, providing a potent support around which a platoon or squad could operate. The tank was very useful, particularly as a 'breaking-in' weapon for Allied advances, but lacked the range of operations or the reliable communications required for a long range 'break-out'. Grenades, trench mortars, gas and improved artillery technology all played important supporting roles.

French unsteadiness and the collapse of Russia in late 1917 offered Germany a window of opportunity to fight on a single front with local superiority. Not to seize this chance in 1918 was unthinkable; while

German Landwehr, armed with obsolete Gewehr 71 rifles, guard Russian prisoners of war. The collapse of the Russian Army following the costly failure of its summer 1917 offensive, and the Bolshevik revolution in October, allowed the best German troops to be transferred to fight in the West.

British strength on the Western Front was set to rise to 1.5 million effectives during 1918, the Americans were arriving and France fought on, Germany was running short of men. Moreover, the Royal and US Navy blockade ensured the dwindling of both food and military supplies to the Central Powers. There were many curious minor miracles with *Ersatz* or 'supplementary' materials: gas masks made of Bulgarian sheep leather, uniforms of shoddy, 'war soap' with sand or clay additives, black pudding 'sausages' and acorn coffee, but the downward spiral towards industrial and literal starvation was clear.

The result was the *Kaiserschlacht* or 'Kaiser Offensive' of spring 1918. Yet, though a break-through was achieved, open warfare gobbled up even more men than trench warfare. Paradoxically there was imminent danger that much more of this success would cost Germany the war. The attack faltered, and the Germans resumed positional warfare. Now it would be the Allies' turn to try to finish the job. The *Materialschlacht* of industrial production had turned in their favour, with tanks and guns sufficient to break the Hindenburg Line and deal the Germans a blow from which they would not recover during the 'hundred days'. Yet Allied victory was not just a matter of numerical preponderance. British infantry tactics were little inferior to those of the enemy, and British tanks were without equal. After initial heavy casualties the Americans learned fast. The Browning machine gun and Browning Automatic Rifle would more than prove their worth. From August 1918 Gen.Pershing had his own sector to fight at St Mihiel, fielding half a million Americans supported by French tanks and aircraft. Later US pressure would be switched to the Argonne.

Much recent debate has revolved around the idea of 'Storm Troops', and whether British or German methods were superior. Yet such discussion tends to obscure rather than enlighten. Most nations had begun experimenting with new assault tactics as soon as their old tactics failed, whether this was the German *Stoss* or shock troops, the British 'grenadier parties', or the Italian 'death companies'. The combatants copied each others' weapons and techniques, and captured and translated their manuals. The 'assault trooper' did not spring from the ether in 1918; and the idea of the German *Sturmbataillone* was not to form a permanent elite, but to make practical experiments before spreading the knowledge acquired through the army as a whole. They were, as Ludendorff put it, 'examples to be imitated'. So it was that following Kalsow's and Rohr's initial efforts in 1915, one *Sturmbataillon* was formed per army during late 1916 and early 1917, sometimes by using the existing divisional *Sturmabteilung* or 'assault detachment' as their raw material. On the

British side, 'Army Schools' of sniping and scouting, bombing, gas, and other specialisms may have been less integrated, and arguably less dynamic; but they were ultimately more successful in achieving a uniform standard of training.

German offensive technique was summed up in *The Attack in Positional Warfare*, a slim volume issued down to battalion level by the Chief of the General Staff in January 1918, with additional amendments later that year. Troops were to be massed for the attack in secret, to penetrate the enemy position 'rapidly', to the 'furthest possible objective' on the *Schwerpunkt* or 'centre of gravity' of the attack, usually on a frontage of 2,000–3,000 metres per division. Overcrowding was to be avoided, though careful preparation might allow initial deployment forward of the enemy barrage zone. Reserves were to be committed on successful sectors, not where resistance was most stubborn.

Artillery preparation would no longer consist of an all-out bombardment lasting days, but was 'concentrated in relation to time and space in order to increase surprise and moral effect'. Trench mortars, infantry guns, and batteries firing over open sights would not be used prior to the day of the attack, so as to maintain surprise. The preface to the assault would last from minutes to hours depending upon circumstances. Pauses, sudden bursts of shells, and the 'fire waltz' back and forth across the target were all useful ruses. During the infantry attack a 'creeping barrage' would move ahead of the troops who would advance, 'immediately behind... in spite of any loss from stray "shorts" and injury to our own men from shell splinters'. The objective was not pure destruction, nor mere weight of metal projected, but *Sturmreifschiessen* – to shoot the enemy into a condition where they were literally 'ripe for attack'.

Artillery was to be co-ordinated at army level to neutralise key points, as had been pioneered by Col. Brüchmuller in 1916 and was now common practice.

Though detailed instructions were to be prepared in advance, and command and control were seen as critical, the manual intended that 'scope for independent action and initiative is left even to the

German infantry wearing variations on 'full marching order'. A mixture of long marching boots and ankle boots with puttees are seen, and one man appears to have improvised gaiters. Gasmask canisters are carried, and several men use bread bag straps round their necks to support their belt equipment.

A message-carrying dog reaches German infantry sheltering in shallow scrapes or shellholes. Note the improvised 'assault packs' worn by the riflemen, with their tent sections rolled and strapped around messtins carried on the back. (IWM Q23697)

private soldier'. This took one stage further the idea of 'directive' command, in which it was the job of senior officers to state the objective, and provide the resources. It was not believed wise to give too many orders, as these would place constraints, and limit the ability of subordinates to take opportunities. Numbers were not the main predicator of success, but quality or 'combat power' achieved by training, equipment, preparation, rest, speed of execution, and intelligence of command and troops.

Seizing the enemy's gun line on the first day, and rapidly bringing up the mass of artillery and fresh infantry, was important. Attacks were generally guided by scouts, followed by assault detachments and skirmishers, but whether 'to employ waves formed of lines of skirmishers or waves of assault detachments, or a combination of both, must be decided according to each particular case'. Where assault detachments were deployed these were often organised in eight-man squads led by an NCO. With the enemy positions thoroughly penetrated the main body of the infantry could follow, feeding the advanced detachments, widening the break-throughs, and destroying the isolated and demoralised pockets of opposition. Each battalion was instructed to take two light *Minenwerfer* forward with it, and in the last year of war *Wurfgrenaten*, or 'jam pot' grenades fired from rifle cup dischargers, filled the gap left by the discontinuation of rodded rifle grenades.

Machine guns were not to be regarded as auxiliary weapons; they were as important to the infantry as the rifle. Close co-operation was vital, with numerous machine guns attached to the lead troops so that 'they may be able to cover the advance of the riflemen and bombers by keeping down the fire from hostile nests, or to repulse hostile counter-attacks'. Light MG08/15 machine gun 'troops' consisting of as few as four men could even be mixed in to form all-arms *Gruppen*. It was readily acknowledged that the élan of the attack might take troops beyond their first objective; but with the understanding that 'the boldest decision is always the best', it was suggested that attacking formations should not be held back unless the advance had become an unconsidered rush.

The individual infantryman's battle was carried out with the *Nahkampfsmittel* or 'weapons of close combat', as described in the German General Staff instruction of 1917. Firearms were supplemented by grenades: blast effect stick grenades, and small iron 'egg' grenades. As the instructions explained, 'The equipment of bombers varies with their task. The following is often

German assault troops take cover in a shellhole. Grenade bags and entrenching tools in improvised carriers are slung round the body; helmets are smeared with mud for camouflage.

'New model' 7.6cm German light *Minenwerfer*, pictured August 1917. Capable of rapid fire and a range of 1,300 metres with high explosive or gas bombs, the 7.6cm was mounted on a traversing plate and fired by means of a pull on a lanyard. The crew shown here includes an NCO and, behind him, a telephonist.

suitable – steel helmet; slung rifle or carbine or pistol; two sandbags containing hand grenades slung round the neck or over both shoulders, or two special hand grenade carriers; entrenching implement; gasmask; haversack with four 'iron rations'; two water bottles; no valise or pouches (cartridges being carried in the pockets or the haversack).'

The men were trained to throw accurately, to long range, and in brief but heavy volleys. When opposed from a trench beyond hand grenade range, bombers were taught to 'close on the trench at all possible speed, throwing their grenades; lie down while the grenades burst, and then rush the trench without hesitation'. Fighting for shellholes or bunkers would normally entail trench mortar, artillery or machine gun preparation and supporting fire during the attack. If resistance continued a machine gun or snipers would fire on enemy loopholes while bombers worked around the flanks.

The German trench mortar 'family' on wheeled carriages, 1918: (left to right) 'new pattern' 7.6cm light; 17cm medium; and 24cm heavy models. Four *Minenwerfer* shells are shown, because the heavy projectile came in two different lengths.

The limitations of a long-barrelled bolt action rifle with a five-round magazine like the standard issue Gewehr 98 in trench fighting and the assault were widely appreciated. Luger P08 and other pistols, trench knives, clubs, and entrenching tools were all used in close combat, but none was ideal in all circumstances. Carbines such as the 98A had been

on issue to specialists since before the war, and their use was extended; but this did nothing to speed operation, or increase the number of rounds in the magazine. Another idea was the development of a 20-round 'trench magazine' for the Gewehr 98; this certainly helped the infantryman to keep firing, and was quite widely used, but was no handier than the ordinary rifle. In 1917 the Prussian War Ministry began a programme to produce a new rifle, while Mauser experimented with a 'trench and close combat' rifle with various sizes of magazine. Neither of these would see general issue, and it was only in the last months of the war that a major break-through was achieved with the deployment of the Maschinenpistole 18.

This was arguably the world's first effective sub-machine gun, a *Kugelspritz* or 'bullet squirter' firing 32 rounds of 9mm pistol ammunition from a 'snail' magazine – first developed for the P08 pistol – on full automatic. Its most effective range was under 50m, and it was capable of causing havoc in the confines of a trench. It was planned to give sub-machine guns to ten per cent of the infantry, but fortunately for the Allies the MP18 would see only very limited distribution before the end of the war.

NEW OFFENSIVE TACTICS – BRITISH

The various editions of *The Training and Employment of Divisions*, published in the last 18 months of the Great War, presented a synthesis of British offensive tactics which were far removed from 1914. While 'general principles' might remain unchanged, methods, application and timing were all drastically revised. Though British tactical plans were arguably less radical than their German counterparts, in that they spoke of 'a methodical and progressive battle, beginning with limited objectives and leading up by gradual stages to an attack on deep objectives' and finally to 'open warfare', the similarities were far greater than the differences. The history of 1/4th Bn Loyal North Lancashires, published as early as 1921, actually claimed that its performance at Third Ypres, for which 16 medals were awarded, 'raised us to the status of Storm Troops'.

Shorter, more responsive artillery bombardments were a key factor. Where bombardments had to be long, aerial photographs now checked progress so that corps commanders

British troops attempt to clear a road across a sea of devastation. This woodland is in a relatively lightly shelled area. In the most heavily bombarded forward areas autumn rains could turn the pulverised ground to a deeply saturated soup of mud, making the movement of infantry and heavy weapons almost impossibly difficult. The third battle of Ypres in autumn 1917 became notorious for the depth of the mud and the frustrating and exhausting difficulty of movement, even when not under direct fire.

could single out undamaged positions for further attention. Guns now used high explosive shells with 'instantaneous' fuses that were capable of bursting on, rather than under, ground level. With better munitions, wire-cutting with shells improved, and efforts were made to keep cleared lanes open during the night by means of rifle and machine gun fire. The objectives of the artillery were similarly more subtle: smoke and gas shoots were mixed with 'box' and 'creeping' barrages, intended to surprise, neutralise or isolate rather than simply to blast the enemy.

Preparing scaling ladders before the battle of Arras, April 1917. 'Toffee apple' trench mortar bombs are visible in the right foreground. (IWM Q6229)

In the ideal barrage plan the majority of the 18pdr field guns would form the creeping barrage, with the attacking infantry advancing about 50 yards behind it. As the manual put it: 'The barrage does not lift direct from one trench to another, but creeps slowly forward, sweeping all the intervening ground in order to deal with any machine guns or riflemen pushed out into shell holes in front of or behind the trenches. This creeping barrage will dwell for a certain time on each definite trench line to be assaulted. The infantry must be trained to follow close behind the barrage from the instant it commences and then, taking advantage of this "dwell", to work up as close as possible to the objective ready to rush it the moment that the barrage lifts.'

Where enemy trench lines were close the infantry would be placed as near as possible, and rush them as artillery fire ceased. With the bulk of the field guns employed on really close work, the 4.5in howitzers and the remainder of the 18pdrs would form a barrage 'in depth', concentrating on strongpoints and working up communication trenches, perhaps with a 'machine gun barrage' superimposed over it. The 60pdrs and other medium and heavy pieces would provide a third barrage, searching the line of advance. Finally, the long range and super-heavy pieces would fire over the objectives, picking out areas where reserves might be gathered for counter-attack or transport routes. Despite the emphasis on intelligent shooting, the British artillery on the Western Front was now firing more shells than ever – anything from one to three million rounds per week from April 1918 to the end of the war.

By 1918 infantry attack was no longer a matter of rigid lines, going in strictly by company and battalion, but a series of more or less flexible 'waves'. The first skirmishing wave followed the barrage into the enemy front line, and homed in on 'points of resistance'; the second, or 'main weight of the attack', came on in platoons of section columns or single file lines. The third wave was 'small handy columns' of reinforcements; and the fourth, troops who were intended to defend the captured

British 9.45in 'flying pig' trench mortar at Pigeon Wood, Gommecourt, March 1917.

territory. The 'files' and 'small columns' were in no way intended as parade ground formations, but loose gaggles – colloquially referred to as 'worms' – taking advantage of the ground. Moreover, as was explained in *The Training and Employment of Platoons*, each platoon now contained within it 'all the weapons with which the infantry soldier is armed – namely rifle and bayonet, Lewis gun, rifle bomb, and bomb'. Each platoon was supposed to have a minimum of 24 and a maximum of 40 men, divided into four sections and a headquarters comprising an officer and three other ranks.

Each section was led by an NCO, and numbered from five to nine other ranks – five being regarded as the minimum number required to work together 'efficiently as a section', and nine the maximum number that could be controlled 'in the conditions of modern battle' by a junior NCO. One section of the platoon was the Lewis gun section, the others rifle sections. Though pretty well everyone was regarded as first and foremost a 'rifleman', all were trained in the use of the bomb, and at least half with the rifle bomb; it was recommended that one of the rifle sections be trained to act as a specialist 'bombing team'. Each section was to be able to provide two men capable of acting as scouts.

Wherever possible men of a section were to be kept together, with drill, fatigues, and team games fostering 'spirit'. Section commanders were encouraged to know the names and characters of every man under their direction. This became more than theory, as an officer of the 8th Bn The Norfolk Regt recorded: 'Men lived, ate, slept and worked in their sections and platoons in which they were to fight in France. Some sections never actually changed between the day of their first formation and the day on which they first suffered casualties in France. The officers not only knew their men by sight and by name, and by their military proficiency, but knew many details of their private lives... Thus was the morale and ésprit de corps of the battalion fostered.'

Though they were expected to co-operate, and provide mutual supporting fire, platoons were now used as tactical units in their own right. In the attack they could advance without halting, but 'leap-frogging' movement was accepted as the norm, with lead troops taking up one objective while others then passed through them and on to the next. Rather than have waves committed specifically to the clearing of linear trenches, dug-outs and 'mopping up', it was now usual to have to clear areas of the battlefield where the enemy were ensconced in shellholes or strong points. Lewis guns aided platoon advances in various ways: directly by firing ahead or to either flank while the riflemen 'leap-frogged', or more covertly by advancing first under cover of night or fog to occupy shellholes or other cover close to the enemy. During major attacks bombing along trenches was now frowned upon, but grenades were used generally for clearing, and rifle bombs as 'section howitzers'. Light trench mortars were expected to be manhandled forward, one or two immediately behind each attacking battalion for support.

Given the apparent modernity of platoon action it is perhaps surprising that the bayonet continued to receive so much attention. Yet it continued to bulk large, at least in preparation for battle, as *Assault Training* spelt out in September 1917: 'The bullet and the bayonet belong to the same parent, the rifle, which is still the deciding factor on the battlefield... It is the spirit of the bayonet that captures the position, and the bullet that holds it. The bullet also shatters the counter attack and kills outside bayonet distance. Bayonet training and musketry training are therefore complementary to one another and must be taught as one subject ... The principles of the assault and counter charge should also be made clear. Throughout the training the instructors should foster the fighting spirit and encourage the desire to kill.'

At the same time it was acknowledged that bayonet fighting was rare: 'Two lines advancing against each other with the bayonet will seldom meet. The one stimulated with the greater fury and confidence, by the force of its determination to conquer, will cause the other line to waver and turn'. This was confirmed by statistics: according to the British official history, just one third of one per cent of casualties were caused by bayonets. The soldiers' contempt for his bayonet was summed up by an entry in *Routine Orders* which noted that many returned to base were found to have lost their temper. Instructions were therefore given that 'on no account are bayonets to be used as pokers or toasting forks, or for any other purpose which will result in their being heated and thus rendered useless as a weapon'.

Gas technology was reaching peak efficiency. From late 1916 British troops were protected with a new 'SBR' or 'Small Box Respirator', which combined an effective face mask with a breathing tube and a box of neutralising granules. By the end of the war Britain had produced in excess of 13 million of these masks, and so effective were they that the US also adopted them. America would make another five million of an 'improved' model, known as the 'CE.' Though they were now better protected, from the summer of 1917 the British were plagued by a highly toxic, persistent and insidious gas which attacked not only the respiratory system and eyes, but burned the skin wherever it touched. Originally this was known as 'HS', standing, it was said, for 'Hun Stuff'. Later the compound was discovered to be dichlorethylsulphide, and became better known as 'mustard gas'. After a

British Indian troops of the 113th Jats prepare to fire No.23 rifle grenades, 1918. Introduced in 1916, the No.23 was a modification of the basic Mills bomb which could be either hand-thrown, or fitted with a rod and used with a ring attachment for rifle projection to a range of about 85 yards. The No.23 was later replaced by the No.36 and cup discharger.

A Royal Engineer demonstrates the use of the No.36 Mills grenade with the cup discharger, 1917. With a range of 240 yards, the discharger was eventually issued on a scale of 96 per battalion. The rifle is held butt to the ground and trigger guard upward, and the grenade inserted into the cup so that the firing lever is confined after the safety pin is removed. It is discharged by firing a bulletless ballistite cartridge.

struggle of some months British chemists replicated it, and the troops replied in kind.

From April 1917 and the action at Vimy Ridge onwards gas shells and cylinders were joined by the more effective 'projector' designed by Capt.W.H. Livens. This was a simple steel tube, standing in a sombrero-shaped base plate, set at a prede-termined angle towards the enemy. By means of electric firing, batteries of Livens Projectors could hurl dozens of large, thin-walled gas bombs into the enemy line to create an instan-taneous cloud. The method was more reliable than cylinder release, able to deliver more gas more quickly than artillery shells, and justly feared. As one German instruction observed: 'The British use this "Gasmine" very cleverly. When the weather conditions are suitable, especially at night, the Projectors are thrown, in a sudden burst of fire, in salvos of six or more, on to our front line trenches. This is usually preceded by an apparently normal bombardment... On account of the effectiveness of this new British Gasmine, the mask will always be carried in the alert position when within 3km of the enemy's trenches, and under no circumstances whatever will it be removed... In addition, working parties, men sleeping in dug-outs, etc., must be protected by gas sentries'.

Tank tactics

Tank tactics made major advances over the last two years of the war. As early as December 1915, Winston Churchill, then First Lord of the Admiralty, had suggested to the War Committee that the new 'caterpillars' should be above all a surprise weapon, for breaking enemy wire 'and the general domination of his firing line'. A more detailed appraisal, submitted by Lt.Col.Swinton to the Committee in February 1916, exhorted that tanks should not be used 'in driblets' but in one great 'combined operation' with the infantry, gas, and smoke. They should be at least a hundred yards apart, with 90 machines advancing on a frontage of about five miles.

Yet Swinton's early aspiration for the tank as a majestic 'break-through' weapon was premature, for unarguable practical reasons. While it had been hoped that the first battle machines might have sufficient mileage to cross the entirety of the German defensive zones in one operation, the actual range of the Mk I tank without refuelling was 23 miles. Moreover, even on good ground the maximum speed was little more than three miles an hour, while start lines, in order to remain even moderately safe and secret, had to be two miles behind the British front. Neither were tanks inviolate: they were very prone to mechanical failure, and as GHQ noted in August 1916, they were vulnerable to shellfire, so were instructed to return to cover as soon as their immediate task was completed. Though the machine gun armament of the Mk I was reasonable, only part of the production, designated 'Male' tanks, carried 6pdr guns. Tank communications were at best haphazard: they depended on waving signal flags or flashing lamps, or – for longer range messaging – on releasing carrier pigeons.

So it was that when C and D Cos of the 'Machine Gun Corps Heavy Branch' were at last committed to the renewed Somme offensive at Flers on 15 September 1916, their impact was local, and their tactics relatively simple. The 32 vehicles which finally made it to the start line were directed to attack specific points in groups or pairs, advancing just ahead of the infantry. They came under the command of the infantry divisions, many of which allotted small parties of troops to act as escort against close assault. Attempts were made to leave clear 'lanes' in the artillery barrage for the tanks.

Given the limited numbers and primitive nature of the equipment it was perhaps surprising that the fledgling tank arm achieved as much as it did in its first battle. Nine machines forged ahead of the infantry and managed to straddle trench lines, interfere with enemy machine guns, or hose down concentrations of enemy troops with their Lewis guns. One machine got all the way to Flers; yet 14 broke down or were ditched, and a total of ten suffered damage from enemy fire. One of these was Lt.Henriques' machine in C Co: 'As we approached the Germans they let fire at us with might and main. At first no damage was done and we retaliated, killing about 20. Then a smash against my flap at the front caused splinters to come in and the blood to pour down my face. Another minute and my driver got the same. Then our prism glass broke to pieces, then another smash, I think it must have been a bomb... The next one wounded my driver so badly we had to stop. By this time I could see nothing at all... How we got back I shall never understand.'

Expansion of the role of the tanks would take time. Only 60 machines were ready for battle at Arras in April 1917, and bad weather and even snow severely hampered operations in which almost every vehicle suffered ditching, breakdown, or damage from enemy shells. In 8 Co of C Bn all ten tanks were disabled, but not before they had succeeded in knocking out several machine guns and snipers' lairs. In 9 Co only five machines would make it into action: of these Lt.Williams' tank had the most hair-raising time, getting 'a whizz-bang [77mm shell] through the conning tower' and ditching twice, prior to being hit by a heavy shell

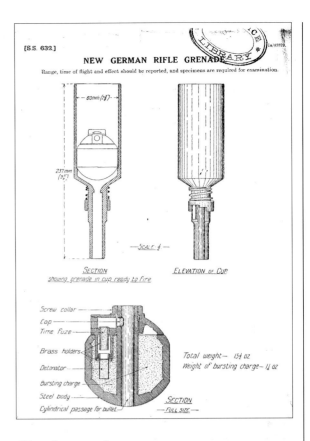

Diagram showing the new German 'Wurf' or rifle grenade and its cup discharger. Like the French VB, on which it was no doubt based, the bomb was launched by firing a bulleted round, which struck the cap and ignited the fuze on its way through the central channel.

which killed three of the crew and wounded three. In 10 Co on Easter Monday the tanks contributed to the attack on Telegraph Hill, but took heavy casualties. Even so, one machine remained in action for the better part of three days, helping the infantry.

In the appalling quagmire of Third Ypres in summer and autumn 1917 tanks were out of their natural element, often sinking into liquid mud until their relevance to modern war was brought into question. Despite acts of heroism the majority were ditched or hit. Just one scene of many was recorded by Col.J.F.C.Fuller: 'I waded up the road, which was swimming a foot or two in slush... The road was a complete shambles and strewn with debris, broken vehicles, dead and dying horses and men; I must have passed hundreds of them as well as bits of men and animals littered everywhere. As I neared Poelcapelle our guns started to fire... the nearest approach to a picture I can give is that it was like standing in the centre of a gigantic Primus stove. As I neared the derelict tanks the scene became truly appalling; wounded men lay drowned in the mud... The nearest tank was a female. Her left sponson doors were open. Out of these protruded four pairs of legs; exhausted and wounded men had sought refuge in this machine, and the dead and dying lay in a jumbled heap inside'.

By the time of Cambrai in November 1917 a new tactical formation known as the 'unicorn' had come into use. A section of three machines advanced in an equilateral triangle, the two rear tanks taking over with them a platoon of infantry in a 'snake' behind them. Cambrai would also see overwhelming numbers of machines used, on reasonable ground, and

Postcard illustration of a wrecked French Schneider tank, and the remains of some of its crew. Early Schneiders were dogged by a lack of spare parts, an alarming susceptibility to German armour-piercing 'K' bullets, and fuel tanks which were prone to ignite. One wonders at the reaction of Fraulein Sophie Cöster of Warburg on receiving this picture from 'her Rudolf'.

The horrific though rarely publicised end of many British tank crews, beside a shell-shattered Mk IV Female tank. Although specifically anti-tank weapons were slow to appear and not very effective, field artillery was a deadly threat.

surprise was achieved with a dawn attack. In all, nine battalions of the enlarged Tank Corps were committed, with a total of 378 fighting tanks. Many of these carried brushwood fascines which were dropped into trenches to provide crossing points. A six-mile hole was punched into German Second Army; but neither exploitation, nor proper co-ordination with the infantry were achieved, with the result that German counter-attacks were able to plug the gap and reclaim much of the ground.

The theory of tank and infantry co-operation was consolidated in *The Training and Employment of Divisions*, where the main characteristics of the fighting tank were defined as mobility, security, and offensive power – what we would still recognise as the armour 'triangle' of speed, armour, and firepower. Yet the Mk IV tank was far from invincible, with a maximum speed of 3.7mph, and armour 12mm thick. According to the manual, this meant that in practical terms the tank was limited to 120 yards per minute on good flat ground, reducing to as little as 15 yards per minute at night. Against a direct hit from a shell the tank was defenceless, but it could expect to be 'proof against all bullets, shrapnel and most splinters'. It could expect to traverse dry shellholes at slow speed, but was in danger of ditching in the wet, and could effectively regard 'swamp, thick woods, streams with marshy banks, or deep sunken roads' as impassable. Artillery was instructed to co-operate more with smoke and counter-battery fire than with heavy bombardments which would lead to cratering.

Infantry co-operation was assumed to depend on mutual understanding of limitations and tactics; comradeship through close acquaintance; combined reconnaissance; and rapid communication. At the beginning of 1918 the last of these was the least practicable, since signalling between tanks and infantry depended on a system of simple semaphore on the part of the troops, and a system of coloured discs on the part of the tanks. A green or red disc signified respecively 'wire cut' or 'wire uncut'; and red and green shown together indicated that the objective had been reached.

German A7V tank 'Adalbert' in transit on a rail flat car, 1918. The A7V had a crew of no less than 18, and mounted one 57mm gun and seven machine guns; five tanks equipped each *Sturmpanzer Abteilung*, of which only three were fully equipped with A7Vs by July 1918. This particular vehicle saw plenty of action. Committed at Villers-Bretonneux in late April 1918 as 'Hagen', it broke down, but was repaired and rechristened 'König Wilhelm'. Under this name it was commanded by Leutnant Heiland during the attack on the River Matz in June 1918, successfully pushing through heavy fighting at Orvillers. When it was decided that the names of royal personages were unsuitable for tanks it was renamed 'Adalbert', going on to serve in the final Marneschutz offensive in July, and at St Etienne. It was finally captured by the French after the Armistice.

Infantrymen requiring the help of tanks held their rifle or helmet above their heads. Wireless signal tanks were still regarded as experimental; vehicles still carried two pigeons for sending messages over longer ranges.

Tank attacks now saw one vehicle allotted to each 100 or 200 yards of front, with a company of 12 to 16 per objective. Sections of four machines were not usually divided. Normally one section of a company acted as an advanced guard while the remainder followed, with each of the following vehicles lending cover to a platoon of infantry going forward in single file sections in its wake. These sections were directed to hold back at least 25 yards as the tanks crossed wire, because it was likely to spring back. On meeting a strongpoint the role of the tanks was to engage, forcing the enemy to seek shelter, distracting and holding them until the infantry came up. The infantry files were instructed to 'move at considerable extension – 50 to 70 yards interval' making 'every use of the ground for cover', the whole attack moving forward 'under the protection of machine gun covering fire'.

German instructions issued in January 1918, shortly before the first use of their A7V tank, were brief but essentially similar. As their *Regulations For the Employment of Assault Tank Detachments* put it, the task of the tank was to support the infantry and demolish obstacles, focusing on strongpoints and machine gun posts. Close contact with the troops was 'of the highest importance', and where necessary sections of engineers were to be attached to help overcome difficult ground. Smoke, night, and other forms of concealment were to be used to hide the German vehicles, and when a mission had been accomplished tanks were instructed to disappear back into cover. German techniques were never thoroughly developed, no doubt because only about 20 of the lumbering, fortress-like A7Vs ever reached the Armoured Assault Detachments; the remainder of the German force comprised captured machines. The majority of these were British Mk.IV tanks, and apart from modification to the armament, as for example mounting MG08 machine guns and some T-Gewehr anti-tank rifles, these *Beute Panzerwagen* ('Booty Tanks') were used much as they had been taken.

A British 3-ton, 55hp Dennis lorry, with Army Service Corps drivers. Expansion in motor vehicle production in Britain and the USA was assisted by pre-war subsidy schemes designed to encourage the introduction of types suitable for the military. In 1914 the ASC had 6,500 all ranks, with 1,200 motor vehicles; by 1918 it had grown to 330,000 personnel, with 47,300 motor vehicles.

Though the British attack never became fully mechanised, the developments in the last few months of the war offered a clue to what armour might one day achieve. 'Whippet' tanks, capable of 8mph and with a radius of action of 80 miles, first saw action in March 1918 and played an important part in the advances of August. Supply tanks, wireless tanks, and tracked gun carriers all saw limited use. Moreover, there was exponential growth in the use of mechanical transport behind the lines.

Merely rotating divisions every two months required the movement of more than a division per day by rail. From late 1916 troop transport trains were typically made up of 50 coaches and trucks, with 1,760 passengers per train. Yet this was just a tiny fraction of the picture, since it was calculated that every mile of the front required 675 tons of stores per day. In October 1916 alone 195,000 tons of stores crossed the Channel from England each week. Much of this was then delivered as train load 'packs' to the front, with each train load made up of a regulation number of wagons of each commodity – e.g. bread, groceries, oats and petrol. Trains were directed to the right divisional railhead by means of colour- or number-coded stickers. In total 76,000 British troops were used to build, repair and run the railways. At the same time there were also light railways, and the War Office was operating 548 craft for inland water transport. Fourth Army alone deployed a motor fleet of 4,671 lorries, 1,145 cars, and 1,636 motorcycles.

Ammunition carriers hitch a ride on a light railway from a shell dump to battery positions behind the front line. Nearly 1,000 miles of track were laid behind the British front during the preparations for major offensives, with more than 520 locomotives and 20,000 wagons under War Department control. (IWM Q5853)

Conclusion

The Great War led to the deaths of about 12 million combatants, a majority of these on the Western Front. Germany lost 1.6 million; France, 1.3 million; Britain and her empire, 900,000. Russia's dead were 1.7 million; Austria-Hungary's, 800,000. The German, Russian, and Austrian Empires passed into history. Britain spent £8,742,000,000, loaning another £1,465,000,000 to her Allies: the 'interim' reparations demanded of Germany were five billion dollars. The horrors of 'The Trenches' led to calls for the abolition of war and a League of Nations. Yet, however catastrophic, 1914–18 was also a war of invention and change.

The Marne in 1914 may have had much in common with the Franco-Prussian War and the American Civil War; but by 1918 the war of material, mass conscription of populations, tanks, aircraft, concrete, and innovative minor tactics would bear more similarity to 1939 than many would care to admit.

THE PLATES

A: BRITISH RAIDERS, 1916–18

A1: Private, 12th Bn East Yorkshire Regiment, January 1918

He is dressed for a winter daytime patrol in the Arleux area. The hooded snow-camouflage 'boiler suit' was provided by the Royal Army Clothing Department to be worn over the service dress. It featured a draw-string around the face, and could be worn with a white helmet cover. Photographs of various regiments show similar suits being worn, under skeleton equipment ('musketry order'), from 1917 onward.

A2: Officer, 1/8th (Irish) Bn, The King's Regiment (Liverpool), April 1916

Photographed after a night raid near Wailly, he has a dark brown private purchase sweater, grey gauntlet gloves, a balaclava, Other Ranks' trousers and puttees; note the slung gas helmet bag. His face is darkened with lamp black. He has a nail-studded trench club tucked into an Other Ranks' web belt, and carries a private purchase Webley-Fosbery .455in revolver. This unusual self-cocking handgun, designed by Col.G.V.Fosbery VC and first produced in 1901, was still carried in small numbers during the war.

A3: Private, York and Lancaster Regiment, January 1918

From a photograph of a patrol ready to go out near Roclincourt on 12 January. The issue 'crawling suit' is worn with a separate caped hood with earslits for improved hearing, and gaiters tightened with straps; the respirator is carried on the chest. In addition to the SMLE rifle he carries regulation wire cutters on a wrist loop, and a No.36 'Mills bomb'.

B: GERMAN ASSAULT TROOPS, 1917

B1 & B2: Flammenwerfer team, 3rd Guard Pioneer Battalion

The battalion's six companies were dispersed in 'troops' attached separately to Sturmbataillone. This team's weapon is the 'Kleif' Model 1916 ('klein Flammenwerfer' – small flame thrower). The equipment weighed 31kg (68lbs), and was capable of about 20 metres' range, having a fuel reservoir of 16 litres (3.5 gallons). B2, directing the projector pipe, wears the old 1910 style uniform, showing the death's-head badge on the cuff as authorised for flame troops in July 1916 – a white badge with black details on a field grey oval. His M1916 helmet is camouflaged with a fitted hessian cover; he carries a slung carbine and a stick grenade, and a photograph shows the pre-war company-coloured bayonet knot still worn. B1, carrying the fuel tank, wears the Bluse uniform jacket authorised in late 1915; he too would wear the death's-head badge on his left cuff. His sidearm is a holstered P08 or 'Luger' semi-automatic. Both men would carry only light personal equipment – water bottles, 'bread bags' and gasmasks. Both display the red-piped black shoulder straps of Pioneers, and the light grey Litzen bars of Guard and some other senior units on the collar.

B3: Leutnant, Assault Battalion

The platoon leader wears an M1916 helmet painted field grey, the M1910 officer's jacket, and field grey breeches with puttees. At his belt he carries three 1916 stick grenades with 5½ second fuzes; his personal weapon is a slung carbine, for which he carries ammunition in his pockets – pouches were often ordered discarded by Sturmtruppen. He is hurling – at a

'My dear parents, a souvenir of the World War 1914–17': a postcard home from a German stretcher-bearer in Flanders. The sender, seated, wears the M1910 uniform jacket; although his collar buttons mark him as only a Gefreiter, note that he follows current NCO practice in wearing a visored field cap. His comrades wear the plainer Bluse jacket introduced in 1915.

bunker or perhaps a tank – a 'concentrated' charge consisting of six grenade heads wired around a complete stick grenade; note that the metal safety cap has been unscrewed from the wooden handle and the fuze initiated by pulling a friction cord before throwing.

C: PORTUGUESE TRENCH MORTAR TEAM, 1917

Portugal entered the war on the Allied side in March 1916, and sent an Expeditionary Force to the Western Front via Britain in January 1917; by the middle of the year this was 40,000 strong. They were partly armed, equipped and trained by the British, with whom they co-operated closely.

C1: Captain, Worcestershire Regiment

This British liaison officer has his regimental badge painted on his helmet, which also has a Cruise mail visor fitted – sliding like a curtain along a wire fitted beneath the front brim with the ends passing up through it to form hooks at each side, it is worn here hooked up out of the way. This specific combination of badge and visor has been observed in a photograph of Capt.E.Jordan dating to March 1918. Under his 'SBR' gasmask bag but over his Service Dress uniform our figure also wears a Franco-British body armour, of small blackened steel scales fixed to a khaki canvas backing. His revolver is the .455in six-shot Webley Mark VI, seen here with the rare Pritchard-Greener bayonet attachment as patented in November 1916.

C2: Private, 23rd Battalion, Portuguese Expeditionary Force
C3: Junior NCO, 19th Battalion, PEF

The Portuguese mortar crew are based on a photograph taken near Neuve Chapelle in June 1917. Both figures wear the national uniform: single-breasted tunic with stand collar and pleated breast pockets, half-breeches and puttees, all in a blue-grey colour similar to French 'horizon blue'. Battalion numbers were displayed in dark blue on the upper sleeves, and NCO ranks by one to four silver stripes on dark blue shoulder strap slides. **C2** has a British helmet and SBR respirator; **C3**, the Portuguese fluted mild steel helmet (made in Birmingham); both wear Portuguese 1911 pattern web equipment – this differed from British 1908 pattern mainly in having only four cartridge pockets on each side. The Stokes mortar had a range of about 800 yards; it has been emplaced here with an additional wooden board under the metal base plate to prevent it sinking into soft ground.

D: BRITISH & AUSTRALIAN SPECIALIST TROOPS, 1918
D1: Driver, Army Service Corps

For comfort during long hours spent almost immobile in the open cab of a supply lorry, he wears the 'Coat Sheepskin Lined' over his Service Dress. The coat was available on a 'Special Scale' of issue to drivers; the Small Box Respirator was a general item for British troops by this time.

D2: Bomber, 1/10th Bn The King's Regiment (Liverpool Scottish), 55th Division

This private of a first line Territorial battalion of The King's Regt displays the 55th (W.Lancashire) Division's red rose sign on both shoulders, a regimental pattern bomber's badge, and a wound stripe on his forearm. He wears the canvas 'Carrier, Hand Grenades, with 10 pockets (Mark I)', over his jacket 'Highland Pattern' with cutaway front skirts, and the regulation khaki 'apron' over his tartan kilt. He is holding a No.27 rifle grenade, an impact-detonated phosphorus type.

D3: Lewis gunner, 29th Battalion, 5th Australian Division

Based on a photograph taken near Warfusée-Lamotte on 8 August 1918. He wears the generously cut Australian version of the Service Dress jacket, with the famous brass Australian Commonwealth Military Forces 'rising sun' collar badge; and on each shoulder a 'colour patch', its shape identifying the division and its colours the battalion. On his left forearm is the wreathed 'LG' skill-at-arms badge of a Lewis gunner. Note the hessian helmet cover; and 1908 webbing equipment, with the head of the entrenching tool moved to the front to rest strategically over a piece of even more personal equipment, in a manner also described in British memoirs.

The canvas 'bucket' carrier for Lewis drum magazines rests at his feet.

E: MISCELLANEOUS GERMAN EQUIPMENT, 1916–18

E1 The 13mm Mauser *'Tank-Gewehr'* of 1918. This unwieldy single-shot weapon, 167cm long and weighing 17.7kg (39lbs), was the world's first anti-tank rifle capable of penetrating any armoured fighting vehicle then in service. Its recoil made firing it a memorable experience.

E2 *Muskete* or Madsen type automatic rifle; overall length 115cm; maximum range 4,400m; feed by 25-round magazine. First deployed in small numbers in late 1915, when three battalions were converted from 4th Bns which existed in some infantry regiments; the first was the former IV/117.Leib Infanterie-Regiment. One battalion was disbanded in 1916; but the weapon was encountered by the British in a defensive role during the Somme fighting of that year.

E3 Loophole plate M1916.

British officers: most are from 2/4th Bn South Lancashire Regiment and display the divisional shoulder insignia of 57th (West Lancashire) Division, a white bar across a red arch. The subaltern at right has three medal ribbons including the MM, and is clearly a commissioned former ranker. So is the second lieutenant from the Worcesters, second from right, who wears the ribbons of both the MC and MM.

E4 M1909 cartridge pouch: a pair – i.e. six pockets – carried 120 rounds of 7.92mm rifle ammunition. Initially brown, but usually dyed black following the new regulations of late 1915.

E5 *Granatenwerfer*, 'grenade thrower'. A spigot mortar with a range of 250m, issued to the infantry and often carried forward in the attack. Overall height about 45cm.

E6 M1916 steel helmet, interior and exterior, seen here with the detachable frontal plate. This was proof against all but close range rifle bullets and was originally intended for widespread issue, but its weight limited its use to what instructions called 'special circumstances'.

E7 The knapsack or *Tornister* Model 1895, interior view, showing compartments for clothing and food. The main compartment measured about 32cm x 30cm x 10cm deep. The oblong buttoned bag was for tent poles, pegs and rope. The early pack had an unshaven cowhide exterior, giving it the nickname 'monkey'. Later examples, like that illustrated, were of field grey canvas with leather detailing.

E8 The *Gewehr 98* Mauser 7.92mm rifle, seen here with the 20-round 'trench magazine'; this modification was not very successful, since the necessarily powerful spring made manual filling difficult. Note bolt and muzzle covers to keep out dirt. Overall length 125cm.

E9 Small signal horn – virtually a miniature version of the bugle – illustrated from a captured example in the Museum of Lancashire.

E10 The issue single-shot flare pistol.

F: FRENCH SPECIALIST TROOPS, 1917–18

F1: Capitaine, Artillerie Spéciale

This tank officer is based on a series of photos taken at Berry-au-Bac in April 1917. He wears the vehicle drivers' black leather coat with cloth-faced collar, which became general issue for tank crews, with his gold rank bars on the forearms. The tank arm (initially designated *Artillerie Spéciale,* and later *Artillerie d'Assaut*) eventually received an adaptation of the standard Adrian helmet, in which the front brim was removed to make it more manageable in confined spaces, and replaced with a leather pad. Out-of-battle headgear was a black beret. Legwear was often a personal option; this captain wears dark blue corduroy half-breeches with leather leggings. He wears belt-and-brace equipment and a map case. The 'Vengeur' trench knife is one of 25,000 ordered in June 1916. The ungainly St Chamond tank, with a 75mm gun, came into use in 1917, serving alongside the Schneider and later Renault models.

F2: Sergent, Transmissions, 8e Régiment de Génie

By November 1918 this regiment was the parent administrative unit for nearly 180 dispersed signal companies and detachments on the Western Front; by April 1916 each division had a 30-man detachment. He is taking down a message over an M1916 field telephone; note his issue pocket watch, and M1892 revolver, lying close at hand. His private purchase *bonnet de police* – of a peaked shape

1917: French 'assault artillery' crew inside a St Chamond tank, armed with a 75mm gun and four machine guns. They have been issued the black leather vehicle driver's coat, but still have the unmodified Adrian helmet.
This photo gives a hint of the gruelling conditions in all World War I tanks: the crews were crammed into a lurching steel box in the narrow gaps between exposed guns and engine, deafened, sickened by fumes, and only partially protected from enemy fire and internal splinters. Production of both the French heavy tank types, the St Chamond and Schneider, was halted in October 1917 to concentrate resources on mass production of the light Renault FT17, which had a better cross-country performance, a two-man crew, and either a 37mm gun or a Hotchkiss MG in a revolving turret.

American 'bombers' advance through wire with sandbags of grenades. The US Army wore British-made steel helmets until contracts could be placed for their own M1917A1 copy with home firms such as Crosby of Buffalo, the American Can Company, Budd, and Worcester Pressed Steel.

popular for some time before its official adoption in 1918 – has black arm-of-service piping (as do his trousers) and a gold braid rank *soutache*. His 1914–15 pattern horizon blue tunic bears regimental collar patches in engineer black with red pipings, and like many NCOs he has added a non-regulation gold number; the sergeant's single gold diagonal bar is worn above both cuffs. On the left upper sleeve below his gold braid one-year front line service chevron is a non-regulation NCO telegraphist's badge – a gold star set against three crossed lightning-bolts. The light brown leggings of 1917 pattern were issued in small numbers to replace puttees. He has general issue pliers in a leather case on his belt; the fluted metal cylinder at his hip is the container for the ARS gasmask developed in 1917.

F3: Machine gunner, 103e Régiment d'Infanterie

This *poilu* wears the buttoned-back, double-breasted greatcoat or *capote* which was the mark of the French soldier in the trenches. Machine gun accessories included a protective mitten for changing hot barrels and a strap-on shoulder pad for carrying, but the latter is not often seen in front line photographs. The air-cooled 8mm M1914 Mitrailleuse Automatique Hotchkiss weighed 24kg (53lbs), and was fed with 30-round rigid ammunition strips. From April 1916 each of a regiment's three battalions had three rifle companies and one MG company. The guns were usually deployed in sections of two, each weapon having a full crew of five; two men loaded and one fired under the direction of the *chef de piece*, while the fifth brought up ammunition.

G: AMERICAN INFANTRY, SUMMER 1918

G1: Private, US 371st Infantry Regiment

This was one of the few African-American units to see combat. Although listed in some sources as forming the 93rd Infantry Division of the American Expeditionary Force, the 369th–372nd Inf Regts never saw action as a complete formation, but were employed separately under French command. Thus the fact that while issued M1912 American uniform these regiments were supplied with blue-painted French Adrian helmets, Lebel or Berthier rifles, and French leather equipment. The 371st reached the Avocourt sector in June 1918, and were committed to the offensive at the Butte de Mesnil in September, distinguishing themselves alongside the French Colonial troops of the 157e Division. In a week of intensive fighting the unit lost 1,052 men killed, wounded or missing – half its strength. The 369th Inf Regt – formerly the 15th NY National Guard, raised in Harlem – had gone into action in April 1918, fighting in Champagne and in the Vosges; according to some sources it was the first Allied unit to actually reach the banks of the Rhine. Under fire for 191 days – longer than any other American unit – it suffered about 1,500 casualties including 367 dead, but never lost a prisoner.

G2 & G3: Automatic rifle team, 137th Infantry Regiment

The Chauchat (CSRG) gunner and loader, dressed in US Army shirtsleeve order with British leather jerkins and respirators, are based on a photo of 'doughboys' of the US 137th Inf Regt, 35th Division, near Amphersbach in August 1918. The firer hunches over the uncomfortably designed automatic rifle, while the loader passes up a semi-circular 20-round magazine; his canvas musette bag holds four magazines. The Chauchat was selected for the AEF because it was available in quantity; but this poorly designed and very crudely made weapon caused endless problems. The system involved the barrel and bolt recoiling together; this long movement caused heavy vibration and thus poor accuracy, and the relative positions of the receiver and butt led to badly bruised faces among its users. The open-sided magazine, its shape necessitated by the big French rimmed 8mm round, positively invited dirt to get into the system, aggravating the already high frequency of jams caused by poor assembly work. A later French-made .30in modification to take the US rifle round was, if anything, worse than the original; and many US troops simply discarded the 'Sho-sho' in disgust.

May 1918: 'doughboys' of the US 77th Div under instruction by a sergeant of the British Machine Gun Corps on the Vickers machine gun. American orders for the Vickers were placed, but it was soon superceded by the M1917 Browning.

H: GERMAN ASSAULT TROOPS, AUTUMN 1918

H1: Sergeant[1], (Bayerisches) 2.Infanterie-Regiment Kronprinz

This section leader from a *Sturmbataillon* formed by a Munich regiment advances with the 9mm MP18 sub-machine gun which was issued in small numbers in the last months of the war. His rank is apparent by the L-shapes of collar lace and the collar side buttons on the M1915 *Bluse*; his state, by the Bavarian checker pattern of the lace. He is lightly equipped, and has small M1889 ammunition pouches on his belt. Black leather equipment and ankle boots were features of the 1915 regulation, formally introduced to the Bavarians on 1 April 1916. Note the 'lozenge' pattern helmet camouflage (also specified for the painting of mortars and artillery pieces), which was announced on 7 July 1918.

H2: Light machine gunner

A sling helps him carry the MG08/15 with its distinctive 100-round drum – this was a belt container, not a true magazine with spring feed for separate rounds. By 1918 this weapon was the main tactical fire support for German infantry; its main weakness compared to the Allied light machine guns was its water-cooled barrel, which made it much heavier. Yet despite its weight of 48.5lbs, manuals suggested that it could be used standing up, or even from trees! The helmet worn is the experimental type with cut-outs over the ears which appeared, together with a questionnaire as to its usefulness, in August 1918. (Its issue after the war mainly to cavalry units of the new Reichswehr has led to the erroneous description 'cavalry pattern'.) The unit designations on the soldier's M1910 uniform shoulder straps are covered with field grey slides.

H3: Unteroffizier, 4.Niederschlesisches Infanterie-Regiment Nr.51

This corporal from a Breslau regiment, his rank indicated by the L-shaped collar lace, prepares to throw an *Eier* or 'egg' bomb. These small grenades could be carried in large numbers, and were commonly hurled over the heads of advancing comrades. This veteran, in old marching boots, covered helmet, and the 1915 uniform, also wears the black wound badge awarded for the first and second wounds; along with the silver and gold classes for higher numbers of wounds, this was first introduced in March 1918.

I: AMERICAN TRENCH FIGHTERS, AUTUMN 1918

I1: Medical orderly

This 'medic' wears the overseas cap and enlisted man's greatcoat, and carries a folding stretcher. His belt equipment, with larger pouches than those of riflemen, is designed to carry field dressings and medical supplies.

I2: Rifle grenadier

This private wears the US M1912 khaki uniform and M1910 webbing set which includes ten ammunition pockets, five on each side of the belt. A 'haversack M1910', canteen set, and gloves dangling from the belt complete his equipment. The M1917 or 'US Enfield' bolt-action rifle is seen here fitted with the French *tromblon VB* grenade discharger, which was also standard issue in the AEF. In the Vivien-Bessière system the grenade was loaded into the cup, and a bulleted round fired from the rifle; this travelled through a central channel in the grenade, simultaneously launching it and igniting the five-second time fuze. Against the tent in the background can also be seen the M1918A1 Browning Automatic Rifle with its distinctive ammunition belt for 20-round box magazines.

I3: Infantry company commander

This captain wears the British type steel helmet with painted

1 Until 1918 this was the German rank between *Unteroffizier* and *Feldwebel*, pronounced *'Schersant'* or *'Schant'*. See p.9, Kurt Hilmar Eitzen, *German-English, English-German Military Dictionary,* Atlantic Press (London, 1957)

rank bars, and the popular raincoat 'for dismounted troops' issued in January 1918. This was constructed of layers of khaki duck material and rubber, and closed with metal snap fasteners. It replaced the old 1910 type poncho, which is seen here in the background serving in its other guise of tent half. The officer's weapons are ideal 'trench sweepers'; slung reversed over his shoulder is a Winchester M1897 pump-action 12-gauge shotgun, and he holds a .45in Colt M1911A1 semi-automatic pistol; this particular handgun is fitted with an unusual private purchase, a London-made 'trench magazine' which would have allowed him to keep firing long after the normal seven-round magazine was exhausted.

J: BRITISH PLATOON ATTACK, 1918

This shows a textbook 'strongpoint assault' against a concrete bunker, using some of the methods outlined in the manuals *The Training and Employment of Platoons*; *Infantry and Tank Cooperation*; and *Training and Employment of Divisions* (1918). While artillery fire cuts off the defenders from reinforcement, a tank crashes through the remaining wire, straddling the trench line and enfilading it with its side-mounted machine guns. Aircraft come in overhead on their way to seek out any counter-attack; in the ground-strafing role to which it was heavily committed in the last months of the war the Sopwith Camel F1 carried four 20lb bombs as well as its fixed armament of two forward-firing .303in Vickers guns.

The infantry platoon, which has advanced by 'blobs' and 'worms' with scouts deployed to the front, now meets resistance and immediately engages the enemy with its Lewis gun section (foreground); the platoon commander takes a vantage point and directs the attack. The

Allied victory parade: French infantry in horizon blue march through London, 1919. Picked from different regiments, they include veterans with double unit citation lanyards, and up to four years' front line service chevrons.

rifle-bombers (right) deploy under cover to one side, and treat the enemy to showers of Mills bombs from their dischargers. The remaining two sections advance in bounds, taking advantage of any dead ground while attempting to work their way behind the bunker. Rifle, bomb, and bayonet will deal with any individuals encountered in the assault. When the final rush is made grenades will be dropped down the bunker steps or thrown through firing ports.

Thillombois, October 1918: American Lt. V.A.Browning firing the .30in M1917 machine gun invented by his father John Moses Browning. A conventional recoil-operated, water-cooled, tripod-mounted weapon in the tradition of the Maxim and Vickers, capable of delivering sustained fire, it was selected as the US Army's principal machine gun in May 1917, and some 27,000 were eventually sent to the AEF. Each three-battalion infantry regiment had a 16-gun MG company; each brigade had a three-company MG battalion, and each division a four-company MG battalion.

INDEX

Figures in **bold** refer to illustrations